DANA SNYMAN

ON THE BACK ROADS

Encounters with people and places

TAFELBERG

Tafelberg
An imprint of NB Publishers
40 Heerengracht, Cape Town, 8000
www.tafelberg.com
© 2008 Dana Snyman

Set in Egyptienne
Book design by Nazli Jacobs
Cover design by Anton Sassenberg
based on a picture taken by Dana Snyman
Translated by Linde Dietrich
Edited by Lynda Gilfillan
Proofread by Lindsay Norman
Illustrations by Dorét Ferreira
Printed and bound by Paarl Print,
Oosterland Street, Paarl, South Africa
First edition, second printing 2009

ISBN 10: 0-6240-04351-7
ISBN 13: 978-0624-04351-5

Acknowledgements

I am grateful to Bun Booyens, editor of *Weg*, for many things. With *Weg*, Bun changed my life. Not only did he give me the opportunity to traverse the country and sit around in small-town bars without feeling guilty – he, more than anyone, taught me to respect words.

Thank you to my publisher, Erika Oosthuysen, for hard work, faith in stories, and the calm with which she persevered, sometimes for days, until she could find me on my cell phone.

I also want to thank all the people who shared their stories with me, from oom Piet Tieties of Swartkop to the dear auntie in Middelpost who gave me a cooked sweet potato to take along for the road.

I am not really one for mottos, but if I had to pick one for this book, it would be from American author Barry Lopez:

> 'The stories people tell have a way of taking care of them. If stories come to you, care for them. And learn to give them away where they are needed. Sometimes a person needs a story more than food.'

Contents

The lessons of the open road

The other night I poured myself a glass of wine and unfolded my rather worn Shell road map of southern Africa on the dining room table. Then, slowly, I started sliding my finger along some of the roads I had travelled in pursuit of stories.

Sometimes a person needs to reflect on things with a road map at hand.

At some point in the past I had circled the names of certain towns – Hoopstad, Migdol and Sannieshof. I can't really remember why. Just as I don't know any more why Heidelberg in Gauteng is heavily underlined.

Next to Colesberg I had scribbled a cellphone number on the map. Whose could it be? I called the number, but a voice said: 'Sorry, the number you have dialled no longer exists . . .'

Maybe it was old Kitte's number – Kitte Honiball, the hobo I'd met in Colesberg at that filling station next to the Merino Lodge.

Sometimes I wonder what has become of Kitte. Just as I wonder what's happened to some of the other people I'd met on my journeys: doctors, farmers, policemen, fencers, flag wavers at road-works, tramps.

I've forgotten many of their names. Or I can't find the notebooks where I'd written them down. Or I find the notebooks, but I can't put faces to the people any more.

I also did a few sums the other night: in the nearly five years I've been working for *Weg* magazine, I've travelled more than 80 000 km per car.

I've been to the Bushveld, the Soutpansberg, the Drakensberg, the Moordenaars Karoo, the Great Karoo, the Little Karoo, the Tankwa Karoo, the Koup, the Koo, the Camdeboo, the Hantam, the Tsitsi-kamma, the Roggeveld, the Richtersveld, the Cape, the Elephant Coast, the West Coast, the Rûens, the Overberg, the Knysna Forest, the Molopo, Gordonia, Namaqualand, the Swartland, Bushmanland, the Lowveld, the Highveld, the Sandveld, the Strandveld, the Free State and Lesotho. I've also visited Namibia, Uganda, Botswana, Zambia and Tanzania.

On one occasion I even went to Secunda.

I've slept in more than two hundred guesthouses and hotels, have told perhaps a thousand petrol attendants: 'Fill up, please!' and at Baardskeerdersbos I was bitten on the foot by a crow.

How many take-away meals have I eaten? Actually, just one, be-cause don't all take-away meals taste the same?

Has the open road taught me anything? What have I learnt? Can travelling change anything in you?

I thought about this for a while. Then I wrote down five lessons that the road has taught me.

LESSON 1: The journey is as important as the destination
Okay, I know it's a cliché, but it happens to be true.

We like to boast about how free we are in this country; and, yes, in terms of the Constitution we are free. But how free are our lives in the city really, hemmed in as we are by burglar alarms, traffic jams, social obligations, shopping expeditions and work pressure?

That's why travelling is probably one of the most enjoyable human activities: the car has been serviced, the suitcases are packed, the provisions prepared. Then, after a struggle to activate the alarm of the house, you and your luggage are in the car.

You are ready to go.

But it's as if the city is a giant octopus determined to clutch you firmly in its tentacles. Nearly all the robots are red, at the filling station the petrol attendant has problems with the card machine, and you have to go looking for another autobank because the one you always use happens to be out of order.

It's as if this is all part of a conspiracy to keep you in the city and prevent you from travelling.

At last you find yourself on the road leading out of the city. The traffic is heavy. In front of you a truck with a load of pigs is trundling along at 35 km/h, behind you there's a road-hog in a Bantam bakkie with a 'banana branch' exhaust system, who thinks a following distance has something to do with rugby.

After a while, the Bantam stops at the back of a queue at a Kentucky Fried Chicken Drive-Thru, and you manage to pass the truck. You relax slightly.

Then, gradually, as the road unfurls ahead of you, you feel a sense of excitement, as if you've just escaped from something that's been preventing you for far too long from being your full, true self. Suddenly, the world is a place filled with almost boundless possibilities.

This is the ecstasy of the open road.

I've discussed this with many people, and just about every one of them can pinpoint the spot where that wordless sense of freedom descends on them whenever they drive out of the city.

A person who lives in Cape Town, for instance, would say that when he travels on the N1, the feeling hits him just after Worcester, at the point where you see the Hex River Mountains looming up ahead. Or if he drives on the N7, the feeling comes upon him among the wheat fields beyond Malmesbury.

The N4 out of Pretoria, the city where I live, is one of my favourite escape routes in the direction of Mpumalanga. Just past Bronkhorstspruit, on the left, there is a poplar grove in open veld. This is the precise spot where I get the feeling.

Then it's time for a Bruce Springsteen CD: 'Tramps like us, baby, we're born to run!' sings The Boss, as the poplars shrink in the rearview mirror and you get comfortable behind the wheel.

These days I prefer to take to the road in my old Mazda bakkie, because it still has the hump at the gear lever in the middle of the cab. You position yourself at a slight angle behind the wheel and rest your left foot on the hump, as you no longer need to use the brake or the clutch.

You drive; now you're driving just for the sake of driving.

Many people also have a specific song they listen to when they drive out of the city.

Our early ancestors led a nomadic existence, which is why we have this deep-seated urge to travel.

Every time you drive out of the city you seem to rediscover this urge within you. This is the opinion of Bruce Chatwin and Larry McMurtry, two of my favourite writers.

It might be silly to wonder about this, but did Piet Retief and Louis Trichardt and the other Voortrekkers of old also get this feeling when they left the Graaff-Reinet area in 1838, the stones crunching under the wheels of their wagons? I think they probably did.

The Thirstland Trekkers, those conservative Afrikaans farmers who trekked away from the old Transvaal in 1875, through the Kalahari and Botswana, up to South West Africa and Angola, seemed to have experienced something of this.

Gustav Preller writes about it in his book *Die Voortrekkers van Suidwes-Afrika*. 'We had a trekking spirit in our hearts that moved us,' Preller quotes one of the Trekkers. 'The reason for this urge to trek couldn't be fathomed. Our homes were tranquil and good. Yet a driving spirit of trekking was in our hearts, and we ourselves could not understand what caused it.'

Today it's possible to travel the highway all the way from Musina to Cape Town and to drive down the main roads of only two towns: Beaufort West and Laingsburg.

Whether you drive from Gauteng to KwaZulu-Natal, or from Cape Town to George, it's the same story: you miss all the towns along the way. And, yes, some people prefer driving from Ultra City to Ultra City to reach their destination as soon as possible.

But that's not travelling. It's driving.

Travelling is stopping at places and opening yourself up to people and things, and, with luck, learning something, or simply enjoying it all and being overawed yet again by this country and its people.

I even had a lesson on love the other day. In Britstown.

A youngster called Loekie Cloete approached me outside the café, with a puppy in his arms. (The café at the filling station in Britstown sells what are probably the tastiest liver patties in the country.)

Loekie wanted to sell me the puppy. 'His dad's a Alstatian, my lanie, a genuine Alstatian,' he said. 'His name's Boendie.'

'Don't you love the puppy?' I inquired.

'Love? Of course I love him, my lanie. But love is mos also just being used to something. I still have four other puppies at home that I'm already used to.'

LESSON 2: Appearances are deceptive

I can never understand it when someone says that absolutely nothing happens in such-and-such a town. That's impossible.

Interesting things happen in all towns (and if there's really nothing on the go, there's always the fashion channel on DStv).

In Karasburg, a sleepy village in the south of Namibia, I once sat watching *Fashion TV* until the early hours of the morning in the company of oom Piet van Dyk, a resident of the town. This was one of the most memorable nights of my life – and not just because the models' clothes were see-through. There were also mutton chops and much laughter, because oom Piet is a repository of funny stories.

I can still hear oom Piet say: 'I also played rugby, ou broer. But I never trained. I sommer farmed myself fit.'

Likewise, I can name the towns one by one where many people would say, 'There's sweet blow-all happening there.'

Richmond, Alldays, Baardskeerdersbos, Paternoster.

At Richmond oom Anneries van Wyk, a retired bricklayer, told me how he had once flown in a Boeing – or a Going, as he called it – to Mozambique.

'I get to that airport, and that Going is standing there with its wings so stiffly on either side,' he recounted. 'You sit and drink tea in it high up there in the sky, and that tea doesn't even make waves in that little glass, it flies so quietly.'

We were sitting on plastic chairs in front of his house. While he told me the story, we drank glass upon glass of guava juice. The previous day a truck with a load of juice had overturned near the town, and some of the residents had sped to the scene of the accident in old cars and collected the containers filled with juice.

Sitting in Richmond drinking guava juice may not be as spectacular as swimming with dolphins in Mozambique, but it's guys like oom Anneries who give a trip its humanity.

There's one thing the open road has taught me: every person has a story – though some do have more interesting stories than others.

At Alldays there's a guy who once shot a kudu while having a conversation on his cellphone. He was driving in the veld in his

14

bakkie, and the kudu just appeared out of the blue. 'Sorry, hang on a bit,' he said to the person he was speaking to. Then he shot the kudu and picked up the cellphone. 'As I was saying . . .'

But it was Kitte Honiball, more than anyone else, who made me realise that on the open road you should never, ever, judge by appearances.

I was on my way to Cape Town when I came across him in Colesberg one morning. He was hitch-hiking to Port Elizabeth, after a narrow escape in Trompsburg: someone had offered him a job. He came up to me at the petrol pump with that trademark request of a tramp: 'Meneer, can you help a guy out with two rand, please?' Then he told me his story.

As he was talking, the sleeve of his jersey pushed up and something on his right wrist caught my eye: prominent scars. Suicide, I thought immediately. At some point life had become too much for Kitte, so he'd slashed his wrists. Unsuccessfully.

He must have seen me staring at the scars, because the next moment he produced a green paper file from his threadbare suitcase. It contained a police statement, sworn to by the commanding officer of the police station at Brits. In the statement he, Kitte Honiball, declared under oath that those scars on his wrist were not caused by a suicide attempt; he'd been helping a man take an old bus apart when the angle grinder he was using slipped, cutting his wrist quite badly.

This was an important lesson for me. Here you have this guy: his clothes are torn, many nights he sleeps under bridges or in parks. Yet his lust for life and his pride are such that he doesn't want someone like me to think that he's tried to commit suicide.

LESSON 3: Sometimes it's not what you see, it's what you hear
People often ask: 'How do you hear interesting stories while travelling? How do you meet interesting people?'

It's easy. Do nothing. Just ask a question or two, then shut up and listen. Good storytellers can be found everywhere, and most of them are very generous with their stories.

It's a good idea to start at the local hotel if you want to find out where the storytellers are. Just remember to take along some coins when you visit the hotel. Nowadays, many bars have a more modern version of the jukebox: you select a song, slip a R2 coin into the slot and press the button.

The other day in the bar at Ventersdorp, a guy came up to me. 'I want all your two-rands,' he said.

'Why?' I asked.

'For the jukebox. I want to listen to "Pampoen" forty-two times.'

How many bars have I sat in, I wonder, and listened to Steve Hofmeyr's 'Pampoen'. At Petrus Steyn in the Free State a chap once asked me: 'Do you know Steve Hofmeyr?'

'No,' I replied.

'Anyway,' he said. 'If you ever see Steve, tell him there's a mistake in "Pampoen". Petrus Steyn doesn't lie on the 506, like he sings. We're on the 302, okay?'

The local old age home, I discover, is also a good place to go looking for stories. An old age home is a library full of living stories.

Will I ever forget the morning in the old age home in Willowmore when tant Marie Nortjé told me about their hard life in the Baviaanskloof in the old days. She was well into her eighties, and on her bedside cabinet there was a note to remind her what day of the week it was: Tuesday.

The smell of boiling meat hung in the air. The tears ran slowly through the wrinkles on tant Marie's cheeks as she spoke about her youth.

You don't easily forget people like that.

I suffer from a serious ailment: I eavesdrop on strangers' conversations. If I'm sitting somewhere and hear two or three people talking, I'm immediately curious about what they're saying. This spices up the open road.

'How old are you, Meisie?'

'Twenty-six, Oom.'

'Do you have any children?'

'Three, Oom.'

'Good heavens, don't you guys have M-Net?'

This brief conversation I overheard in Warrenton. Or could it have been Windsorton?

Something has just occurred to me: maybe I underlined Heidelberg on my map to remind me of what I once heard the manageress of a restaurant say to a client who was out to cause trouble.

'Stop your nonsense,' she told him. 'This place belongs to a Portuguese. I just press a button, and all the Portuguese in town will come here to beat you up!'

I remember wondering how Heidelberg's male Portuguese population would arrive. Would each man come in his own car? Or would just one Toyota Dyna truck pull up with all the guys on the back, geared up for action?

It's like this that you get to hear a brief chapter out of people's lives. You don't know what happened before. You don't know what happened afterwards.

I only visited Heidelberg – Heidelberg in Gauteng – on one other occasion, and that time I also heard something that I won't forget. This was in the hotel, the old Heidelberg Hotel that no longer exists.

I was eating a bar lunch there. A few guys were standing at the counter. After a while, two of them started arguing. I couldn't hear what the argument was about, but it probably involved women, rugby or cars.

The two guys were getting more and more cross with each other. One of them was quite smartly dressed in a pair of brown Clarks shoes, long trousers, a white shirt, and a Mickey Mouse tie.

Then, all of a sudden, they started hitting each other with angry, white-knuckled fists. And while the fists were flying, one of them shouted at the guy with the Mickey Mouse tie: 'You'd never say you're the manager of Russells!'

Not so long ago, I stopped at a filling station in Secunda. At that moment a man came walking out of the building, followed by two youngish girls. The man looked annoyed. The three of them got into a souped-up Opel Astra and the guy drove off with screeching tyres. Ear-splitting.

And then the petrol attendant, who'd also been watching this little scene, suddenly said next to me: 'There go Mister Van Tonder and his daughters.'

End of chapter. You fill your tank and drive to the next town.

Once, a truck driver sat next to me at a bar counter in Bloemhof. I was reading a newspaper, and he was deep in thought. This was obvious. He had a heavy frown between his brows and was moving his cigarette lighter in slow circles around the ashtray in front of him on the counter.

Suddenly he stopped and looked at me. 'Have you ever reversed an Interliner?' he asked angrily. 'Hey? Have you ever reversed an Interliner?'

Soon after that, he got up and left.

What could have happened? Had he perhaps reversed his truck over a car? Or maybe even a person?

I'll never know. End of chapter.

LESSON 4: Sometimes you find stories without looking for them

I appreciate the value of a GPS navigator. It's a useful instrument, but I prefer for the most part to travel without one.

In the city you are never allowed to forget where you are. Everywhere, you are surrounded by signs: the names of streets, suburbs, office blocks, flats. And when at last you manage to escape from the city, do you still want to know, down to the degrees of longitude and latitude, exactly where you are? It's usually not necessary.

To me, travelling means surrendering myself to the rhythm of the open road, yet without forgetting the ultimate destination.

Because I'm constantly on the lookout for stories and interesting people, I have also learnt this: if you open yourself up to stories, they will come looking for you.

Once I drove from Cape Town in the direction of the Overberg without any idea of what I was going to do there. At Baardskeerdersbos I stopped at a building with the sign: *Boeredanse elke Saterdagaand* (Barn dances every Saturday night).

As I got out of the car, I heard a child inside singing: '*Skipskop, Skipskop, wanneer hou die dinge dan op . . .*' (Skipskop, Skipskop, when are these things going to stop . . .) – David Kramer's well-known song.

I went inside. The singer was the small daughter of the owner, Danie Groenewald. I sat down at the counter. The next moment, the oom next to me asked: 'Did you know that Skipskop is a place?'

I then heard Skipskop's story: how it was once a fishing village near Waenhuiskrans, how all the residents, white and coloured, were forced to move to make way for a missile-testing range.

Danie invited me to his dad's house for a snoekbraai. (It was at oom Manie's that the pet crow later bit me on the heel.) After that, I began searching for people who'd once lived in Skipskop. Most of them now live in Stilbaai, I discovered. And almost all have photos in their drawers, dog-eared with frequent handling.

This was a journey that will always make me look at the Overberg and its people with different eyes.

And then there was the girl called Linda.

She approached me one night at the Formula One Hotel in Bloemfontein. I was spending the night there on my way home to Pretoria from somewhere or other. (Formula One hotels are veritable treasure chests for stories, particularly because so many reps stay at them.)

Could she have a lift with me the next day to her sister in Germiston, this Linda girl asked. I was sceptical. I'd read lots of newspaper stories about a girl that asks a guy for a lift. Then there's a guy who's in cahoots with her, and the whole Bonnie-and-Clyde thing happens.

In the end, though, she convinced me. She had an honours degree in Afrikaans literature. She had just been divorced from her husband.

She slept most of the way. I dropped her at her sister's house in Germiston and didn't hear from her again.

Until about a year ago.

On that particular day, my car was being serviced in the centre of Pretoria and I was wandering through the streets to pass the time. Suddenly a girl approached me. She looked vaguely familiar. With her was a big chap who looked like a Nigerian. She greeted me. She was thin to the point of anorexia and there were sores on her face. Her eyes were vacant.

It was Linda. Drugs had consumed her.

After that she phoned me once from a tickey-box. She was incoherent and said something about a Nigerian she worked for. Since then I haven't heard from her again.

Yes, the open road also opens you to sorrow.

LESSON 5: A journey is never really over

We have all experienced journeys that we talk about for years, even decades afterwards. Do you remember that time the elephant chased us in Etosha? Do you remember the time that the wave in Margate sent Ouma tumbling, in her crimplene dress?

Again and again I find myself sitting on a sofa in someone's lounge, inspecting a photo album while being told about a trip.

We repeat our journeys again and again in our imagination.

Just put your finger anywhere on a map, and so often a name will dislodge all kinds of memories.

Wesselsbron. Dust and grain elevators, on the way to Bloemfontein.

Keetmanshoop. My late mother sitting in our Valiant with a migraine and saying to the petrol attendant: 'Please bring the ounooi a Cream Soda, my jong.'

Welkom. Seagulls at a roadhouse. (A certain gull species is indeed found in Welkom.)

And then there are the people I sometimes think of: Kitte, Linda, the guy with the Interliner. There are many of them.

In May I was in Tanzania. One morning the photographer, Ruvan Boshoff, a Tanzanian and I were driving through a small village in the south of the country. Suddenly something caught my eye: four men were walking on the pavement, carrying a shabby bier on their shoulders. On the bier lay a corpse, swaddled in a sheet. They were on their way to bury the corpse and couldn't afford a coffin. Some of the men weren't even wearing shoes.

It's a picture that has stuck in my mind: the men, the weak morning light falling on the bier, the stony pavement.

We are all equal in our mortality.

Maybe I'm hopelessly idealistic, but I believe that on every journey subtle changes occur within you, provided you open yourself up to what happens around you.

Once I wrote down a quotation in one of my notebooks. The other night, while I was poring over the map at the dining-room table, I reread these words and perhaps really understood them for the first time.

'A man sets out to draw the world,' writes Borges. 'As the years go by, he peoples it with images of provinces, kingdoms, mountains, bays, ships, islands, fishes, rooms, instruments, horses and individuals. A short time before he dies, he discovers that his map traces the lineaments of his own face.'

By travelling, we discover not only this beautiful, awe-inspiring earth; we also discover our humanity, and that of others.

I'll always be a traveller.

Miami Village, St Helena Bay

Japie Fourie points angrily to the spot where a crane had earlier unloaded an enormous palm tree from a truck. 'Can you believe it, ou bggroer?' he says, pronouncing his r's with the typical burr of the region. 'Now they're planting palm trees.'

We are near St Helena Bay on the Cape West Coast. Soon this area will boast a collection of identical houses behind a high fence. 'And do you know what they're going to call the place?' asks Japie. 'Miami Village.'

Miami Village, St Helena Bay, South Africa – next to towns such as Goedverwacht, Graafwater and Eendekuil.

'Unbelievable.' Japie kicks at a stone with one of his Nugget-deprived shoes. 'Un-be-liev-able! Nowadays there are more bloody builders than bushes on the West Coast.'

That's a fact indeed. There are few other areas in the country with so many property developments mushrooming all over. You soon discover this when you take the R27 – the West Coast road – from Cape Town along the coast, past Melkbosstrand, Gansekraal, Yzerfontein, Langebaan and Saldanha, to St Helena Bay.

Everywhere, you see the patches of land cleared for building, the golf courses in the making, the Tuscan villas, the Bali houses, the Boere-baroque I-have-a million-in-the-bank houses, the huge billboards with colourful photographs and enticing promises:

Come and experience the spirit of the West Coast.

Amazing views from every room.

Beaches dotted with palm trees.

And, yes, all of this looks rather out of place in this region of small fishing boats and diamond divers, of storyteller Tolla van der Merwe's yarns and singer Worsie Visser's jolly ditties; the region of fynbos and all kinds of unusual flowers: snapdragons, golden showers, kanonpypies and chincherinchees.

This is where you come to eat crayfish and snoek and fish of all kinds. Here you drink Golden Valley wine and are held spellbound by the voices of people you meet – characters with nicknames like Ben Koggelman, Koos Krap and Frikkie Rooitou. Hospitable folk who speak with a burr and come up with all kinds of stories and wisecracks.

Like the guy at the filling station in Langebaan who this morning said: 'He has so many freckles, he looks like a calendar full of public holidays.'

Or people such as Japie, born and bred on the West Coast, at whose place I stopped here at Shelly Point.

'You won't believe me, bggroer,' he says, 'but at the age of sixteen I knew only two English words: Ford and Mobil.'

Now, suddenly, there are places in the vicinity with names like Miami Village, Bay View Mountain Retreat, Capri, Blue Lagoon and Paradise Beach.

Don't just buy a home, buy a lifestyle.

Security estate in Langebaan with a country feeling.

Wake up every morning looking through God's window.

24

'There's no doubt about it,' says Japie. 'Your real, true West Coast is disappearing.'

One of my mom's cousins, Buks Griesel, was still alive the last time I paid a proper visit to the West Coast. This was in 1997 or '98. He and his wife, tant Kittie, had lived in Saldanha for donkey's years.

Oom Buks also spoke with a burr, smoked Life cigarettes and occasionally drank Lieberstein wine. When he liked something, he would shout: 'Apples! Apples!' On Fridays he sometimes said: 'Today is Friday, pay day, drink-and-fight day.'

'Old Buks is very *earthy*,' my mom used to say politely. 'West Coast people are so earthy, aren't they.'

'What does earthy mean, Ma?' I asked her once. She didn't quite know how to answer my question.

'It means that oom Buks likes to go barefoot,' my dad said.

Now oom Buks lies buried in Saldanha's cemetery, and dear tant Kittie is in a home for the aged in George.

From Miami Village I drive in the direction of Shelly Point and Paternoster, because Japie Fourie reckons that if there's still a true West Coast left, it's at Paternoster.

These days, Shelly Point, too, has palm trees and a golf course – together with the accompanying exotic promises, of course.

Watch the glorious sunset from your own patio.

Beautiful family home in a cul-de-sac.

Face-brick delight.

Shelly Point is also home to the Vasco da Gama Nautical Museum. I stop there and get out of my car. The museum is divided into two parts, without a separating door: one part is the museum, the other an estate agent's office. While I'm busy looking at an exhibition on the Cape Khoi people in the seventeenth century, a woman in a tailored suit is selling a house to someone over the telephone in the office section. 'Yes, sweetie . . . yes . . . Fab, it's absolutely fab . . . Yes . . .'

I get back into the car and wonder why so many estate agents wear their dark glasses on the forehead – even indoors. Perhaps to be specially prepared in the event of a quick deal.

I sometimes wish that, like other people, I could just drive into a town and accept things as they are – without stopping everywhere and asking questions, without being drawn to museums and cemeteries and bars, trying to find out how things are and how they were, wondering why they no longer are the way they were.

Maybe it's just that today I miss those days when I was eleven years old and we visited oom Buks and tant Kittie in Saldanha. Oom Buks always used to braai kob on the coals, and tant Kittie baked foil-wrapped sweet potatoes in the oven, and once a friend of oom Buks took us out on the lagoon in his boat.

A Protea Hotel now stands on the spot where we got into the boat.

I drive away from Shelly Point. The area around here is also known as Agterbaai. You can drive straight from here to Paternoster on a dirt road. Or you can take the tarred road via Vredenburg. I take the dirt road.

Is this perhaps the road where a local character, Dirk Kotze, driving his Ford Fairmont GT one night, caused a Lewis delivery bakkie to overturn?

The story goes that Dirk's Fairmont had broken down. Then the fellow in the Lewis bakkie offered to tow him. They'd barely set off when Dirk turned the Fairmont's key, and the engine started. Then, rather absent-mindedly, Dirk decided to overtake the bakkie . . .

Not very long ago, Paternoster was still something of a secret. The road to the town was untarred. It was just a place with a lot of fisherman's cottages, a hotel, and a shop with a Coke sign on the gable.

Today there are four estate agencies, and some of those fisherman's cottages are worth more than R1 million each.

An undiscovered dream.

While sipping sundowners, watch the whales and dolphins frolic.

The office of one of the estate agents, Johan Jansen van Vuuren, is next to the Paternoster Hotel. 'Do you see those houses?' He points to the rather modest houses on the foreshore. 'They're now selling for R3 million each.'

This is reason enough for me to flee to the hotel.

It's now just past four in the afternoon, and two men are sitting in their own cloud of smoke in the bar. On the ceiling above their heads hangs a larger selection of female underwear than you would find in Pep Stores in Vredenburg: bras, panties, G-strings.

One of the guys, a salesman from Cape Town, tells me that these days he repeatedly watches his wedding video. 'But I watch it in reverse,' he says. 'I watch how my wife and I are standing in front of the pulpit. Then I watch how I reverse back into the vestry and how she reverses out of the church and out of my bloody life . . .'

'Apples!' my oom Buks would have shouted at this point. 'Apples!'

For the first time since leaving Cape Town, I feel as if I'm on the West Coast that echoes with Tolla van der Merwe's stories.

The hotel was built in the 1940s and has been in the possession of Johan Carosini, a well-known personality of the West Coast, since 1973. Today, Johan is rather quiet. There was great sadness here at the hotel just a week ago because Sokkas, his ancient Labrador, had to be put down.

Everywhere against the walls of the bar and the hotel, both well-known and lesser-known visitors have signed their names and written messages: Bles Bridges, Worsie Visser, Ernie Els, Anton Goosen, Gé Korsten. Someone from the Drakensberg Boys' Choir also signed – on behalf of them all. (One signature looks as if the name could be Ossie Gibson. Maybe it's the one-time TV reporter, Ossie Gibson, I wonder aloud, but Johan Carosini isn't sure whether Ossie was ever here.)

'Anton Goosen was the first person who signed here, in 1978,' says Johan. 'Gé Korsten was here fourteen days before his death.'

A few years ago, Johan got into hot water on account of the women's undies hanging in the bar. A policeman confiscated fifty-eight panties and G-strings. But the case was withdrawn. Now the underwear is hanging here once again, as a kind of testimonial of the West Coast's earthiness.

'I requested the panties from guys who came here on their honeymoon,' he says. 'It was those guys who gave them to me.'

A tall man enters the bar. Barefoot. Rooies Enslin is his name. 'Give me an Oros, pal,' he says to the barman. 'With a straw.'

'It's genuine Oros,' says Neels van Zyl, who is sitting on the stool next to mine. 'Genuine-genuine Oros.'

Rooies looks at me almost apologetically. 'I don't drink during the day,' he explains. 'I'm a builder.'

It's almost midnight, and I'm still in the bar of the Paternoster Hotel. The stories are coming in thick and fast, like the snoek run here in December. Dirk and Mona Venter are here, too. They come from Richards Bay, and for the past fourteen years they have visited the hotel each February for a two-week stay in Room 3. Apparently Sokkas, the hotel's Labrador, had come to know them so well that he'd start whining as soon as he saw them.

'Sokkas once greeted Mona with his paw,' says Dirk.

'Genuine-genuine-genuine,' confirms Neels van Zyl, a Pretorian now living in Paternoster.

Sokkas's intelligence and abilities, you discover, increase as the evening progresses. Just a moment ago, someone claimed that the old dog could kick a soccer ball nearly twenty metres.

According to Bennie Groenewald, Sokkas once even started barking when the WP rugby team scored a try against the Blue Bulls, while they were watching here on TV.

'Genuine-genuine-genuine,' Neels confirms again.

Tonight I've come to discover a few things, here in the bar:

- Fanta Orange is known here as Jannie-verjaar-koeldrank.
- A big snoek is called a bokwa.
- Paternoster has another name, too: Smokkelnoster. Right in front of the hotel is a dune known as smuggler's dune. Sometimes, the fisherfolk stand on the dune among bluegums blown skew by the wind. When you drive past, they lie one hand on the other and flap-flap-flap, like a crayfish flapping its tail. Here, you can buy an illegal crayfish. Not that all crayfish you buy here are illegal, though. The fishermen are given crayfish quotas, and those crayfish you are permitted to buy. But these days the quotas are pretty meagre.
- Almost everyone on the West Coast claims to have known Worsie Visser personally. Naturally, Neels van Zyl knew him too. 'We were great pals, old Worsie and I – genuine-genuine-genuine,' he says. 'Did you know that Worsie made his big money with diamond diving? In '91 he dived out a helluva parcel right here.'
- An undertaker in the district has a sticker at the back of his hearse that reads: *Arrive Alive*.
- Not all West Coast people speak English equally well. As Johan Carosini puts it: 'Here we use English only in self-defence.'

Apparently oom Drikus Smit was sitting here the other night when an English-speaking woman came into the bar, clearly upset and in tears. She and her husband – they'd come here on holiday from Cape Town – had had an argument. Then she told her sad story to oom Drikus, a prim and proper oompie whose English was abysmal.

Nevertheless, oom Drikus listened attentively to the woman. After a while, she evidently asked him: 'What advice would you give me, Oom? What must I do?'

Then oom Drikus gave her some good, fatherly advice. In his best

English: 'Lady, all I can say to you is just keep jou kant clean.'(Keep your nose clean.)

Just after midnight, I excuse myself and leave the Paternoster Hotel. It's time to go to bed. The sea lies as peacefully as Psalm 23 in the moonlight. I stand on the stoep for a while. Neels van Zyl joins me. He's a former helicopter pilot who'd decided eleven years before to sell everything in Pretoria, move to Paternoster and make a living from carpentry.

'Here you become human again,' he says, the tip of his cigarette glowing red in the dark.

How long does he think the Paternoster Hotel will survive, I ask. After all, this is prime land.

Do you want a piece of heaven? Don't delay.

'I don't even want to think about anything like that,' says Neels. 'I don't even want to think about it.'

It's not that all the old West Coast people are opposed to development. Johan Carosini is one of those who welcome it. It's good for the community, he says. It benefits everyone.

But there are also some who reckon that it's still a case of the haves getting even more, and the have-nots continuing to struggle, as in the past. And on top of this, most of the expensive houses here don't even belong to people who are permanent residents. The owners only come to the area for weekends or holidays.

Great invesment opportunity.

Sun-filled dreams.

Towns such as Langebaan, Saldanha and Vredenburg are expanding. And it seems as if a lot of West Coasters who make money are spending it on sound systems for their cars. A local newspaper, *Die Swartland & Weskus Herald*, regularly publishes letters from people complaining about this noise.

'My house is on the corner of two busy streets, and I often have to soothe my frightened little boy during the night,' writes Cannot Sleep from Saldanha. 'The racket made by the people who come thump! thump! thump! round the corner is as good as a hi-fi suddenly being switched on in your lounge.'

It's true. I'm now here in Vredenburg, and have just spotted a thump-thump-thumping Toyota Corolla. I go closer. The guy behind the wheel is Mervin Cloete, a factory worker, and I hear the term 'op die pif' for the first time.

When you're 'op die pif', you drive nice and slow, sitting low in the seat of your car with one arm out the window (often with your cap back to front) – a sight often seen on the West Coast roads.

This is the best way to travel on the West Coast, I decide. Go 'op die pif' – but without the noise. Sit low, drive, and wonder what my oom Buks would have done if he'd seen what is happening on the West Coast nowadays.

Experience a movie-star lifestyle with yachts on your doorstep.

Now I'm on my way to Laaiplek and Velddrif. Or as the people in these parts pronounce it: 'Velleghuf'.

Velddrif is where the Berg River flows into the sea. There are more than 240 bird species here, as well as, well, a Loch Ness pig. There are rumours going around about a pig that lives in the river – one that can swim underwater. Apparently some fishermen have seen it and have heard it snorting under their boats. Genuine-genuine-genuine.

Here, there also all kinds of developments, especially at Port Owen near the river mouth.

Tuscan mansion overlooking the marina, beautiful views and beautiful sunsets.

Eigelaar. It's a surname you hear and see everywhere in Velddrif. The Eigelaars are probably the town's best-known family – fishermen who were penniless when they started out and became wealthy through hard work: oom Johnnie and oom Enrie, oom Floors, oom Albert, oom James and tannie Edna.

A few years ago oom Johnnie wrote a book, *As die skipper op die voorstewe staan*, where he tells the story of the Eigelaars and a large part of the West Coast's fishing industry, too.

Oom Johnnie is seventy-seven years old and his health is not all that good. Yet affluence hasn't driven him to one of the Tuscan villas. He and his wife, tant Sannie, have lived for years in the same face-brick house with two ship's anchors outside the door, in River Street in Laaiplek.

It's early afternoon when tant Sannie opens the door for me. Oom Johnnie doesn't speak much. The old man's memory isn't so clear any more. He sits in the lounge with his hands resting in his lap – hands that for years pulled nets up from the sea, snapped off the heads of snoek, and gutted fish.

'When last were you in Saldanha?' he asks.

'This morning, Oom,' I reply.

Oom Johnnie doesn't respond. He's the last of his generation here on the West Coast. He used to go out to sea with so-called bakkies – small fishing boats – and catch fish that were sold by the basket.

Oom Jannie is apparently also able to identify all kinds of things with a 'kontrepsie' he has made from wire and a copper pipe. 'At night I stood on the bow of the ship and pointed out schools of fish with it,' he writes in his book. 'With the wires I can also point out abalone in the water, as well as abalone that is in the freezer. When a woman is six weeks pregnant, I can point that out as well.'

It's time for me to go.

'When last were you in Saldanha?' oom Johnnie asks again.

'This morning, Oom.'

Again, oom Jannie doesn't respond.

He and tannie Sannie accompany me to the stoep. 'Pick a rose to take with you,' she says. I select a rose – a red one.

'You probably know what that means,' she says.

'What, Tannie?'

'Love.'

The name of their house is Uitkyk, but these days they can't see very far because so many houses have been built between them and the sea.

Storybook residence.

32

Stunning sea view.

Location, location, location.

North of Velddrif, the landscape becomes even emptier, less violated. And then, about 30 km on, there's a signpost: Dwarskersbos. With a property development a short distance away.

Picturesque house that pleases the heart.

Your search is over.

Not far from Dwarskersbos is the small beach at Soverby. All that remains here are the remnants of a few fish tanks. Yet this was once one of the busiest fishing spots on the West Coast.

Here, the fishermen had what they called 'trekke' – men like oom Japie and oom Floors and oom Ben Theart. A trek is a fairly sizeable area in the sea where grey mullet especially were found in abundance.

They say that a strong fellow called Jampa van Dyk once won two hundred bokkoms here at Soverby in a wager. It seems he'd bet the fishermen that he could pick up a sand-filled grain bag with his teeth. Then he did it.

Just beyond Dwarskersbos, the tarred road peters out into dirt and the pretentious names and promises disappear for a while. In the distance, Bobbejaansberg forms a hump on the horizon.

My cellphone beeps in my pocket. It's an SMS from Neels van Zyl of Paternoster: 'Dirk Kotze has bought a new Nissan Hardbody. He reckons the thing is so fast, he's already three instalments in arrears and he hasn't even got into the car.'

At the Elandsbaai Hotel the air is thick with gloom.

A girl with a parrot on her shoulder is sitting quietly on the steps. Then the door at reception swings open and another girl runs out. 'Tell your damn boyfriend he must stop phoning here!' she shouts at someone in the kitchen.

This is one of the best-known old hotels on the West Coast. I make for the bar, where someone's artificial leg hangs from the ceiling. At the door, two fair-sized suitcases and some folded blankets await collection.

The barmaid has a half-completed *Huisgenoot* crossword in front of her. Her name is Marietjie Cronjé. She doesn't feel like talking. When I ask her whose artificial leg is hanging from the ceiling, she merely says: 'It belonged to an oom who drank a lot.' Then, a while later, she adds, 'He's dead now.'

More time passes, and then a woman comes into the bar. 'Your family has arrived,' she says to Marietjie. They embrace. A tear is Kleenexed from a cheek.

Only then do I hear the news: the Elandsbaai Hotel will be closing in two days' time. Boetie Nel and his wife Sonja, the current tenants, have decided to throw in the towel after more than eight years.

Outside, Marietjie loads her suitcases and blankets into the boot of a Camry. They slowly drive off.

No one stands in front of the hotel to wave goodbye.

Fanie Cloete has to hurry. The guys are waiting for him in their small fishing boat, ready to go out to sea. But he first wants to fetch his dog.

'Flaffie!' he calls, and runs through the shallow water to where some five or six dogs have gathered on the sand to see the boat off. 'Come, Flaffie! Come!'

He bends down, picks up a 'pavement special' from among the group of dogs, runs back into the sea, and jumps into the boat with the dog in his arms. Flaffie goes out to sea with them daily.

It's just past eight the next morning and I'm here at Doringbaai, about 120 km north of Elands Bay. Yesterday afternoon, feeling rather sad about the closing of the Elandsbaai Hotel, I drove here via Lamberts Bay and spent the night at the municipal resort.

I look at the picture before me here at the harbour: Fanie with Flaffie in his arms, the little boats, the rowing teams, and all the other dogs that have come to see their masters off.

'When last were you in Saldanha?' I hear oom Johnnie Eigelaar ask again.

34

Tant Sannie's rose still lies on the seat in my car.

At Doringbaai they only fish on a small scale these days. Most of the fishing people now work for big companies that own big boats with all kinds of modern equipment.

What's more, the fishermen are currently involved in a dispute with the government about the allocation of fishing and crayfish quotas. The Department of Environmental Affairs and Tourism had apparently received more than four thousand applications from people wanting to catch crayfish – and only seven hundred were approved.

The quotas are valid for ten years. The people who didn't receive quotas must wait until this period has lapsed before they can re-apply.

'They're killing us,' says Johnnie April, one of the fishermen who couldn't get a quota. 'Tell me, what are we supposed to do? Start smuggling crayfish?'

Last night I wrote a quotation from the American writer William Kittredge in my notebook: 'A sense of place is bound up to some degree with the way people are in that place and with the history of the people, and it's bound up even more with physical and natural detail, with trees and grass and soil, weather, water, sky, the way some weeds smell when you walk on them. These are the details of place, and an awareness of them is what I call a sense of place.'

In the past few days, the West Coast's history and bushes and sky and crayfish have spoken to me through Johnnie April and Johan Carosini, Rooies Enslin, Japie Fourie and tant Sannie Eigelaar – and also through my memories of my oom Buks.

The details of place are also there in the stories about Jampa van Dyk's legendary muscular strength, Dirk Kotze's Fairmont GT, and oom Drikus of Paternoster's sparse English. And for as long as these stories are told, the West Coast will always be there in some way.

But the West Coast is also changing. It's a fact. That's life.

When last were you in Saldanha?

'Our trek has run out'

That day, oom Piet and tant Grieta had stood for a long time next to their donkey's grave at the roadside. First oom Piet prayed, and tant Grieta, wearing a bonnet as usual, wiped away a tear. Then the two old people sang a psalm – one that was worthy of the late Cradock.

He'd been a hard-working donkey, old Cradock.

'A donkey is the Lord's animal,' says oom Piet. 'You pay a donkey your respects.'

Next to him tant Grieta nods. 'And you dig a deep hole for him, otherwise the stink comes out at the top and that stink comes after you.'

The two old people are sitting in the hollows of a wobbly sofa outside their shack at Swartkop, about 250 km north of Calvinia.

'Did you and tant Grieta bury *all* your donkeys in this way?' I ask oom Piet. 'Or just old Cradock?'

'Every single one of them.'

Their donkeys have always been their most prized possessions. Oom Piet and tant Grieta Tieties are karretjiemense – as they're known around here. The karretjiemense have had a nomadic existence for many generations. They trek from farm to farm with their

36

donkey carts, in times of hardship and in times of prosperity, kilometre after kilometre, whether to shear sheep, mend fences or do odd jobs.

At night they sleep next to their carts under the stars, only to pack up again and carry on trekking, like gypsies.

Karoo gypsies. Afrikaans people.

I sit on a green melamine chair opposite oom Piet and tant Grieta. I look at them as they gaze over the flat, grey shrubland, and wonder if they don't perhaps have a picture of themselves at Cradock's graveside.

'Didn't Oom ever take photographs?'

'How? With what, Meneer?'

I'm travelling through the Karoo in search of karretjiemense, and this is the response I get from all of them: they have no photographs – except for those on their identity documents.

'I was born on the road, in the region of Carnarvon,' says oom Piet. 'My late father sheared sheep there. But then the sheep-shearing ran out. So we came trekking along here, past Prieska, Marydale, those parts. A month here, a month there . . .'

Yet this is a way of life that has all but vanished, because nowadays oom Piet and tant Grieta are camped out here at Swartkop more or less permanently. They've even put up a little shack of corrugated iron, stones, clay and the bumper of an old Chev car.

Off to one side, a donkey cart rests on its shaft.

'But I still have my donkeys,' says oom Piet. 'I'll always have my donkeys. One of these days I want to go to Strydenburg.'

The old man likes talking about his donkeys – both living and dead. And when he talks, you shut up and listen, because oom Piet's speech is poetry.

Die Jirre was goed vir my. Ek't al rêrig sielige donkies gehet. Hulle dood net op, die donkies, en dan sit jy met die hart se breek. (The Lord has been good to me. I've had donkeys with real soul. But they die, the donkeys, and then you sit with the heartbreak.)

Nowadays, it's hard to find karretjiemense who still trek from farm to farm. Those I've managed to track down don't really trek any more. They live in townships in Hopetown and Strydenburg, as well as here in Swartkop, where I'm chatting to oom Piet and tant Grieta.

'You see, our trek ran out,' says oom Piet. 'The world now is . . . it's different.'

There are good reasons why the karretjiemense aren't trekking any more: there is little work for a nomadic sheep shearer or fence mender like oom Piet. Farmers have their own shearers, or they go and pick up shearers in the townships in their bakkies. And a Bloemfontein fence-making business can achieve more in a day than an elderly oompie like Piet can manage in a week with a pair of pliers.

In the Karoo these days, there are also fewer farmers, on bigger farms. Besides, the roads are fenced off. You can no longer just outspan anywhere you like, and it's hard to find enough grazing for your donkeys, goats and chickens.

But the urge to trek still stirs in the karretjiemense I spoke to: Blom Links and Jan Louw from Hopetown, Klokkie and the Smeer family from Strydenburg, Jantjie Links from Pouvlei; and oom Piet and tant Grieta here at Swartkop.

'I can harness those donkeys in front of that cart right now. Now, right now.' Oom Piet motions to his cart with a knobbly hand. 'Then I can hit the road.'

'Where do you find karretjiemense who still move around full-time?' I ask. 'Or doesn't anyone trek any more?'

Oom Piet becomes quiet. The wrinkles on his face are like the roads on a map. He has also buried donkeys at Prieska, Draghoender and Kleinbegin. He points to the south.

'Go and look at Vanwyksvlei,' he says. 'Some there still trek around.'

Vanwyksvlei is about 80 km from Swartkop. I take my leave of oom Piet and tant Grieta and turn the Condor's nose in that direction – soontoe, or syntoe, as they say in these parts.

It's a dirt road. Today, Barry Manilow is the Afrikaans radio station's music icon of the day. As I listen to RSG, I try to picture old Barry, with his white sequined suit, white shoes and coiffed hair in front of his white grand piano, in this bare landscape, free of all frills and ostentation – and immediately switch off the Condor's radio.

Everywhere, the donkey-cart tracks snake across the road. To and fro they wind, but nowhere is a karretjie to be seen.

The karretjiemense usually trek in a convoy of four or five donkey carts, carrying all their possessions with them. Some carts carry chickens, and sometimes even a meek goat. And invariably a dusty dog trots alongside, with its pink tongue hanging out (I would find out in the next couple of days that many of those dogs are called Oortjies).

At night, it's not just a simple case of outspanning and making up a bed on the ground. On each karretjie you'll find a few pieces of corrugated iron and wooden poles, which are deftly erected around the karretjie, almost like the tent of a caravan. And then the karretjiemense crawl in under their makeshift shelter for the night.

If you ask around, you'll find that there's always been a reasonably good relationship between the karretjiemense and the farmers. A competent shearer can shear between fifty and seventy sheep a day. For each sheep shorn, they're paid R2,60. Sometimes the farmers help with the delivery of babies, and in transporting the sick to hospital.

No one knows for sure how many karretjiemense there still are in the Karoo. Or, rather, no one knows for sure how many people there still are in the Karoo who regard themselves as karretjiemense.

Professor Mike de Jongh of Unisa's anthropology department has been studying the karretjiemense for years, and he reckons that there are at most a thousand left. Almost all of them now live in townships on the fringes of Karoo towns.

The younger generation is increasingly alienated from the older generation's way of life. They look for jobs in the towns, and some even head for the cities.

As Piet Tieties rather poetically puts it:

Op die pad is daar altyd beterskap voor
toe gaan die beterskap weg;
nou sit ons hier, en trek
in onse gedagtes

(On the road there was always something better ahead, then that disappeared; now we sit here, and trek in our thoughts.)

Early in the evening I drive a bit bumpily into Vanwyksvlei, somewhat disappointed because I couldn't find the karretjie that had made those winding tracks.

In the main road, the Wynvat café has already closed. The lights of the Dutch Reformed Church are on, however, and eight Toyota bakkies, one Tata and an old Kadett are parked on the pavement outside. A pentecostal service is being held there tonight.

I'm the only guest at the hotel.

The next morning I get an important lesson from Hendrik September about building donkey carts. A donkey cart, for those who don't know, consists of roughly seven parts: the wheels, the axle and springs, the floor, the sides, the seat, the splashboard (where the passengers on the seat rest their legs), and the shaft.

I track Hendrik down in the township. It's not his karretjie that made yesterday's meandering tracks on the Swartkop road, because he'd outspanned here in his family's yard more than a month ago.

He points to his donkey cart standing askew in a clearing. Soon, he promises, he'll yoke his donkeys to his karretjie and hit the road. To Prieska. There are jobs there, they say.

An old man and old woman, stooped over their kieries, approach us from the direction of the shack. Three children come running up over the veld.

The old man is wearing Grasshoppers that were possibly grey before this rugged part of the world got hold of them. This is some-

40

thing that never ceases to amaze me: the impact of a particular landscape on the shoes of its inhabitants. Shoes in these parts age differently from, say, Lowveld shoes. Or Mossel Bay shoes. Or Free State shoes.

The old couple and the children come and stand with Hendrik and me. Mickey Mouse peeps out from among the stains on the shirt one of the boys is wearing. The words 'Hi folks!' are faintly visible.

They say nothing, the old people and the children, and just stand listening to Hendrik as if they're witnesses on his behalf.

'I built this cart myself,' Hendrik says, walking around his donkey cart with a dog at his heels. 'The rims I got from a guy in Copperton. They belonged to an Opel that crashed. The tyres come from Jantjie Bruinders, but I don't know where he got them from.'

Someone must have thrown those two tyres away, because they are completely worn.

'And the springs?' I ask. 'Where did you get those?'

'These springs, Meneer, these springs belonged to oompie Klaas Louw, then he mos died, oompie Klaas. Then old tant Siena said I can just as well come and take them, there's nothing she can do with them.

'This piece of corrugated iron here at the bottom comes from Brandvlei. There's a place near there called Rondomlelik. I went and picked it up there, this sinkietjie. I think the children played doll's house with it. Before that it was maybe part of a farm dam or a windmill's tail or something.'

Hendrik rubs the right side of the karretjie. 'This side here, I think this side comes from the old café in town – the Sonskyn café. It was one of the signs there.'

He may be right, because the letters 'Sonsk' can be deciphered on the side.

'The left side I picked up in Calvinia at the rubbish dump. It might have been a door or something.'

He points to the seat. 'This plank here was an old cupboard of mine that broke. But it broke as if it had to, Meneer, because then I took it and sawed it a bit and made a seat for this cart of mine.'

Next to me, the old man and old woman nod solemnly. It's all true, what he says. That's how it happened.

And so, while we stand and listen, Hendrik September relates how all these loose parts from all over the district came together, almost like an act of faith, to become a donkey cart in Vanwyksvlei.

I say goodbye and drive further south to Vosburg, about 120 km from Vanwyskvlei along a reasonably good dirt road. In Vosburg, Hendrik said, there might still be a few karretjiemense.

The woman at the shop in Vosburg directs me to Karel Malgas in the township. But oom Karel, who was born and bred on the road, doesn't even have donkeys any more.

He, in turn, directs me to Sampie Smeer, but Sampie, too, has bid the road farewell. One chilly winter's night, he took his donkey cart apart, sold the wheels, axle and shaft, and used the rest for firewood.

'Try Britstown,' he says. 'That lot still trek.'

On the pavement in Britstown's main road, I walk past a woman carrying a parrot in a cage. A poster in a shop window advertises a thanksgiving festival in Orania, not far from here. Pancakes and pudding will be on sale, and you can also take part in a target-shooting competition.

'Whose parrot is that?' I ask the woman. She eyes me warily, as if she suspects me of wanting to kidnap the bird.

'It's the meneer's parrot,' she says firmly. 'I'm taking him home.'

I ask a man at the café about the karretjiemense and he points down the road. 'They're there in the Noodkamp.'

The Noodkamp (emergency camp) is a squatter camp on the edge of the town. Next to one corrugated iron shack, two donkeys stand in the classic donkey-resting position: legs close together, head down, eyes closed, motionless.

I stop. A man approaches me. Petrus Syster. Yes, he is one of the karretjiemense, but, 'Ag, I don't really trek any more. I just use the donkeys and the cart to fetch wood.'

He points to eight or nine shacks standing next to a bare, uneven soccer field, almost like alien spaceships from a joyless planet that have landed here.

The Noodkamp.

'This used to be our temporary outspan,' Petrus explains, 'but now we just stay here all the time. The trek has run out.'

A movement catches my eye: from among the shacks a young boy comes running, barefoot. In his hand is a piece of plastic that he twisted into a line, and tied to a kite – a kite he has made himself with pieces of reed, plastic and wire.

The child runs as fast as he can across the soccer field, but the kite refuses to take off. It just drags behind him on the ground.

There are many people with the surname Syster in the Noodkamp: Petrus and Jantjie, Dirk, Sakkie and old oom Jacob – and their families. The Systers have been karretjiemense for donkey's years. And from time to time, some of them are still picked up by farmers to shear sheep.

It's virtually impossible to say when the first karretjiemense started trekking through the Karoo, or when they first called themselves such. Once upon a time, in the eighteenth century, just about all the Karoo's inhabitants, white and brown, were nomadic trekkers who moved around with their livestock. But in time, farms were demarcated and fenced off, farmsteads were built, and farming enterprises were established.

And then, especially for those who couldn't afford land or weren't allowed to own it, the trek road beckoned, from farm to farm, kilometre after kilometre, in good times and bad times.

That was the beginning of the Karoo gypsies.

I've arrived at oom Jacob Syster's corrugated iron shack. As with all the other shacks here, there's a donkey cart in the clean-swept yard. Drieka, oom Jacob's wife, sits on a chair that has no back to it. At her feet lies a dog that's so thin, it's almost as if you could play a piano tune on its ribs.

Tant Drieka speaks in a whisper. 'My old husband is inside. He's very ill.' She motions to the shack behind her.

'What's the matter with the oom?' I ask.

'Ag, he's just feeble.'

'How old is he?'

'He's old, Meneer. He's already off the calendar.'

Tant Drieka is full of stories of the road. One of her children, Sakkie, was born under bright Karoo stars next to a donkey cart.

'The donkey cart shook Sakkie loose.' Tant Drieka laughs. 'I just went and lay down there on the ground, then he came, and we clothed him in some small things and then everything was beautiful.'

They also had plenty of fun on the road. 'It was different then,' she says. 'We didn't have tapes for music. The old ones had guitars, they played those guitars until they fell apart. And we danced, ooh, wild, wild, wild!'

The boy with the kite is still running to and fro across the soccer field among the corrugated iron shacks, but the stupid kite doesn't want to take off. It keeps dragging behind the boy.

A while later, I enter oom Jacob Syster's shack. It's twilight here, there's no window. A thin beam of light shines through a hole in the roof and forms a bright spot on oom Jacob's shoulder.

His body is a small pile of bones under a colourful Pep Stores blanket, and there's something wild in his eyes. He's spent most of his life on the trek road, always moving. He greets me in a soft voice.

One can't help thinking that oom Jacob is on the final stretch of another trek. 'Has Meneer been to De Aar?' he asks suddenly, almost inaudibly.

'I have, Oom.'

But the old man doesn't say anything more. On the small table next to him stands a jar of Vicks. I try to think of something to say to him. 'Did Oom own good donkeys in Oom's life?' I ask.

'I had many good donkeys in my life, Meneer.'

I go back outside, just in time to see the boy come running across the soccer field once again. In the meantime he has put on shoes, perhaps so that he can pick up more speed.

He holds the kite's plastic rope high above his head, and he runs, and he runs, faster and faster. And then it happens, one of the most beautiful things I have ever seen: that homemade kite takes off. Higher and higher it goes.

The further the child runs, the more it looks as if he's running away from this damned Noodkamp, away from tattered clothes and cold water and drunken oompies who menace each other with Okapi knives late on a Saturday night.

He's running away from dry bread and corrugated iron shacks and diseases that make people thin and cause them to cough throughout the night.

He's running away from memories of dead donkeys and all the hardship of a life between somewhere and nowhere, while the kite rises above his head, and keeps rising.

I'm now headed for Kraankuil, a dilapidated railway halt in the Barry Manilow-unfriendly open flats north-east of Britstown.

Here, there are apparently still karretjiemense who trek from place to place. That's what Abraham Visagie has just told me. He and some of his friends were travelling in a horse-drawn cart next to the road near Britstown, and I stopped to talk to them. They are farm labourers, but Abraham was wearing a brand-new police cap.

'Are you a policeman?' I wanted to know.

'No, I picked the cap up next to the road. I think the policeman was drunk, so it blew away.'

'Go and look in "die gang" at Kraankuil,' Abraham also said. 'That's where the karretjiemense are.'

Die gang. The corridor. It's a term you often hear among the karretjiemense. 'We're trekking down die gang,' one might say. Or: 'We made camp in die gang.'

Die gang is the long stretch of land on either side of a fenced-off road or a railway line. Some karrietjiemense also talk of die langplaas (the long farm).

Kraankuil's gang is on either side of the R388 between Hopetown and De Aar. Near the old station buildings and pepper trees I see it: corrugated iron shacks next to the road, with people, and donkeys, and dogs – eight, nine, ten dogs, small ones, big ones, brown ones, spotted ones.

A spotted dog charges at me, all teeth, as I get out of the car.

'Sie jy, Oortjies!' a man calls. Jantjie Blok is his name. He and his wife, Marie, and their children have been camping out here more or less permanently for more than a year.

Now and again they inspan the donkeys and ride to Hopetown to go to the shop, but they no longer wander around as they did in the old days. Jantjie does odd jobs on the farms around here. At first he used to ride around on a thick-wheeled bicycle, but now the bike hangs in pieces from the branches of a tree next to their shack.

'I broke up the bicycle,' he explains. 'Then I left it to hang there for a bit, because the children were riding too much. But I'll build it again. It's been hanging for too long.'

Oortjies growls at me again. Jantjie shoos him away and introduces the other seven dogs to me: 'That one is Kolletjie, and that one is Storm. And that one there on the karretjie is Hartseer.'

'Why is his name Hartseer?' I ask. Sadness.

'Because he's totally fierce, Meneer.'

The other day, Hartseer helped Jantjie to catch a porcupine – for the pot. Some of the other karretjiemense have also told me how much they like porcupine meat. 'First you take out all those quills in the boiling water,' says Jantjie. 'Then you scrape him clean with a knife. Then you boil him in a pot over the fire.'

'How long?' I ask.

'Just about three hours,' Jantjie replies, but Marie chips in: 'It depends on how old the porcupine is.'

As with any other community, it's impossible to generalise about the karretjiemense. Some are pious Christian people who read the Bible every night and sing psalms and hymns by candlelight, but there are also those who are hard of heart.

There are the diligent and the less diligent, the cheerful ones and also the sombre ones who spend their days sitting on upside-down paraffin tins in the shade of a pepper tree with their heads full of dark thoughts.

There are also the drinkers who, late on a Saturday night in a township shebeen, sometimes pull an Okapi knife from a trouser pocket and flick it open in anger.

I'm now headed via De Aar, Philipstown and Hanover to Coles-berg, because in Colesberg, Jantjie Blok of Kraankuil said, there are karretjiemense who still trek around.

But I'm now beginning to wonder about that story. Maybe, I decide, karretjiemense like Jantjie simply want to believe that some-where, some place, there are still some of them who live the old, free life.

In De Aar, Philipstown and Hanover it's more or less the same story: the karretjiemense's trek has ended in the township. And those who still own donkey carts are now required, would you be-lieve it, to register their carts with the Northern Cape Traffic De-partment, and to have a number plate and a reflecting board on the back to prevent cars from driving into them at night.

There is an age-old legend in these parts that is still told. I first heard it when I was about seven years old and lived in Daniëls-kuil in the Northern Cape.

One day, the story goes, there was a horrible accident somewhere around here: a man in a car drove straight into a donkey cart. The donkeys and everybody in the donkey cart died, and the shaft of the cart went right through the driver of the car.

But the man in the car didn't die. He sat there, alive, with the shaft sticking through his body and the back of his seat. They say he was still able to chat and joke with the people who came to help him.

Then, very carefully, they started pulling the shaft out of the man. But just as they managed to remove it, he died on the spot.

If you approach Colesberg on the N1 from the direction of Cape Town, you will see a One Stop petrol station and restaurant on your left. Just behind that is the Merino Lodge.

Turn left there, and take the dirt road that passes towards the right of the One Stop and the Merino Lodge. About 2 km further on, you'll see a row of shacks in the gang to one side of the road.

Here is another group of karretjiemense: Dina Cloete and Jan Louw, Kerneels Smeer and his wife Doortjie, and others, some younger, some older, and children rolling bicycle tyres along and kicking dead soccer balls – and a collection of dogs and chickens.

Painted in big letters on one of the shacks is: *7de Laan Straat*. This is what they call their ramshackle outspan.

I stop the car. Dina Cloete comes up to me. 'It was a beautiful life,' she says later about the old trekking days. 'It was a good life.'

Now they just sit here. But still, this life also has its advantages. After all, there's a school nearby for the children, and a clinic for the old and the sick. There's also a tap with running water, and at least once a week a pastor holds a prayer meeting for them all.

These are all privileges which they never really had on the road. Above one of the huts, a TV antenna points skywards. Nowadays they can even watch TV. 'We watch *7de Laan*,' confesses tant Dina.

A youngish man comes closer, his breath smelling of sweet wine. 'Can Meneer please help us with one thing,' he says. 'We want a sign here next to the road that tells people they should drive slowly, because they're killing our dogs.'

The other night while they were holding their prayer meeting, a bakkie sped past here. There was the sound of brakes and a dog yelping.

It was old Piet Cloete's dog. It was Willehond's last yelp.

I decide to take a group photo of all the karretjiemense near the One Stop. Colesberg probably has the biggest community of karretjiemense who don't trek any more.

'Come! Come! Come!' Piet Cloete calls. 'We're going to take a kiekie!'

Then some of the people come closer: Tant Dina with her colourful headscarf, and oom Jan Louw with his shaky old legs.

Piet Cloete fetches his two chickens to pose with him.

The young guy with the sweet-wine breath stands apart, sombre.

Kerneels Smeer brings a plastic bucket to sit on.

Gert Syster holds an ostrich he's made from a pine cone and pieces of wire.

Two boys roll bicycle wheels closer.

Everyone takes up position in front of a shack. I turn the lens in their direction.

Some smile. Some frown and stare straight ahead. Others look sombre, almost sad.

I look at them through the lens – the last of the karretjiemense.

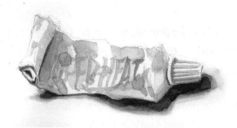

Deap Heat and deserted fields

It's a dismal picture: the pavilion's paint is flaking and the scoreboard is rusty. Even the rugby posts are missing from the field. The change-room windows are broken, and inside it smells of Jeyes Fluid and dust. And lost dreams.

It's been a long time since a rugby match was played here on the municipal field of Ventersdorp, in the old Western Transvaal. Or so it seems.

I get back into the car and drive further into the town. I stop at the Madeira café because the oom at the Caltex filling station had told me earlier that the Madeira's owner, Rian Visser, is a rugby player.

Indeed: Rian is a flank – a flank without a team. 'Earlier this year we still jolled,' he says, 'but we can't get enough guys together any more.'

They'd played three matches, against Leeudoringstad, Koster and Potchefstroom's second team – and lost all three. Then the guys started with their excuses: knees that suddenly played up, necks that became stiff overnight, asthma, you name it.

He shakes his head. 'Some guys are pretty slapgat, if you ask me.'

Is this the situation too in other platteland towns nowadays, I wonder. Is adult rugby still being played, not just school rugby? Real, proper rugby.

Do some spectators still park their cars next to the field on Saturday afternoons and hoot when the teams run onto the field, or a player scores?

Do tannies still bake pancakes and jaffles on small gas stoves behind the pavilion? Does the change room still smell of Deep Heat before the match, and of Old Spice afterwards? Do platteland players still pray in a little circle before and after the game?

Whether in the north, west or south, almost every South African town once had a rugby team – even dorpies such as Marydale, Daniëlskuil and Tarkastad. Velddrif. Pofadder. Clocolan.

Here in Coligny, about 50 km from Ventersdorp, there was once more than one team. Right until the late 1980s, this town was an important railway link, with a bustling railway station. There were lots of guys here who loved rugby.

Nowadays, hardly any trains shunt at night, and turkeys scratch for food in the goal area of the municipal rugby field.

I stop near the posts. The local racing-pigeon club has taken over the clubhouse. A man approaches, accompanied by a yapping dog: Phillip Botha and Lassie (a dachshund, not a collie as in the movies).

Suddenly, I remember another distinctive feature of a platteland rugby match: an exuberant mutt would usually run a few circles on the field during the game. It generally belonged to one of the players, which often meant quite a struggle to remove the animal from the field.

Oom Phillip believes what many rugby fans do: there's a connection between the decline of platteland rugby and the constant bungling of the Springboks and our Super 14 teams during the past decade.

This might be a simplification, but one thing is certainly true: the platteland used to be – and to a degree still is – the breeding ground of Springboks, dozens of them. Legends such as Mannetjies Roux (Victoria West), Piet Visagie (Beeshoek) and Danie Gerber

(Despatch) carried on playing for town teams even when they were Springboks.

Once upon a time there was also an SA Platteland Team that regularly played against overseas teams and in '81 even toured South America, beating Paraguay, Uruguay and Chile.

Coligny, however, hasn't produced any Springboks. (Though the town did present Hestrie Cloete as a gift both to the world of high jump – and to Jurie Els.) I walk across the field, turkeys scuttling off ahead of me. Was it perhaps here in Coligny that a referee one Saturday afternoon awarded a penalty before kick-off?

One of the teams ran onto the field, the story goes, and a player had the ball in his hand. Then he passed it – but too forcefully – and hit the referee against the head. The referee summarily awarded a penalty kick on the centre spot to the other team, without the game having been kicked off.

But oom Phillip knows nothing of this incident. Many platteland rugby stories have become legends, but it's hard to establish where the events took place, and whether the tales are in fact true.

Johan van der Walt is seated on a low wall in front of the Nice liquor store in Biesiesvlei, some 30 km from Coligny, sucking on a cigarette as if it holds all the solutions to his town's rugby problems.

Biesiesvlei's rugby field has reverted to veld.

'I think they took the posts to Lichtenburg,' says Johan through a cloud of smoke, and shrugs his shoulders. 'Or maybe they're in Sannieshof.'

The distance to Sannieshof is about 20 km. I drive to the town, but no one I ask knows anything about Biesievlei's posts. It also doesn't seem as if rugby is played here at all any longer. Someone directs me to the local mill, but the people there don't know anything about a rugby team either.

I press on to the next town, Delareyville, where, to all outward appearances, the rugby situation is similar. The Dries Venter stadium is on the edge of the town, and signs of decay are clearly visible. 'Shitsvally Stadium' has been spray-painted against the pavilion by someone with a slight spelling problem.

As I drive further into Delareyville, I wonder who this Dries Venter might be.

Small-town rugby fields often have names like this: the Dries Venter stadium, the Boetie Posthumus stadium (Colesberg), the Fanie de Bruyn stadium (Kroonstad).

In the main street, one name jumps out at me: Bokkie's Cylinder Heads. The name has a bit of a rugby sound to it. But Bokkie shakes his head when I question him. 'You should talk to Klein-Munro at North West Tractor Services,' he says. 'He plays rugby. He'll probably know who Dries Venter is.'

On the pavement, a certain Clint informs me that the town used to have a rugby team, but they had too much trouble trying to get players. Many tales about platteland rugby involve unending struggles to scrape together the full complement of players for teams.

It is said that Christie Hammond, secretary of the Robertson rugby club, once even stopped next to two hitch-hikers before a match against Montagu.

'Okay, guys,' he is said to have told them, 'you can get a ride, but first you have to play for us.' In the end, the hitch-hikers turned out for one of Robertson's teams.

I drive to North West Tractor Services. Klein-Munro Swanepoel is the son of Munro Swanepoel, a businessman from Delareyville, and yes, he plays rugby, but for Ottosdal, a neighbouring town, because Delareyville no longer has a team.

The biggest problem of platteland rugby, says Klein-Munro, is money. Jerseys and other equipment aren't cheap. And if you're injured, you have to pay your own doctor's bills. A knee operation can easily cost you R15 000.

He walks into a small, empty office. A bag filled with white-and-green rugby jerseys lies in the corner. These were the jerseys of the Delareyville XV in the days when they still played; now they just lie there in the dust, a forlorn monument to platteland rugby.

I am still in Delareyville. Klein-Munro has given me directions to Louis Venter – he's the son of oom Dries Venter, after whom the town stadium is named.

Louis, who works at Karoo-Osche Auctioneers, himself played for Delareyville in his day. 'We were a rugby family,' he says. 'My dad was also one of the founders of Delareyville's rugby club and Stella-land Rugby Union. He now lives in Lichtenburg.'

He goes off to rummage in the drawers of his desk and returns with a 'remembrance' his sister Elize once wrote about their dad. With this in hand, I drive back to the Dries Venter stadium. Again I park next to the field, and get out of the car. Behind the northern try line is a row of bluegums, and in the open space between something that looks like meerkat holes. This is the place where oom Dries Venter had once put in so much effort.

I remember how my dad used to go and open the sprayers to water the field in the mornings before going to Western Ford (he was the manager there), wrote Elize in the 'remembrance'. *My sister, brother or I – or whoever was wandering about nearby – always had to help him move the pipes. It was a blessed nuisance.*

I walk across the withered field and stop on the centre spot. An empty beer can lies near the ten-metre line.

Bonzo, our lion-coloured ridgeback, always knew immediately when my dad got into his white Ford Fairlane and drove to the rugby field. Taking a shortcut past the tennis courts, Bonzo would follow my dad's car at breakneck speed. Sometimes he wandered off and first chased a few meerkats.

Here, like in Coligny, the clubhouse has been taken over by the racing-pigeon club.

When my dad had finished, Bonzo would get into the Fairlane with him (back seat) and my dad would drop him at home. One Saturday afternoon, Ferdie Strauss of Schweizer-Reneke and his cronies stole Bonzo after a match. Delareyville and Schweizer had played against each other. My dad was very upset, and drove all the way to Schweizer to fetch Bonzo.

Not all platteland rugby clubs have their own clubhouse, which is why the lounge or ladies' bar of the local hotel often serves as the clubhouse. Here in Vryburg, which still has a town team, the guys often hang out at the Elgro Hotel.

Many platteland rugby stories are hotel stories. Like those involving Toy Dannhauser, former Transvaal lock, who was the manager of the hotel in Clocolan in the Free State in the 1980s. On more than one occasion, it's reported, he allowed male guests, some with minimal rugby skills, to sleep in the hotel for free in exchange for playing for the town team.

Clocolan once turned out on the field without a lock, and oom Toy apparently persuaded the referee to scrum for them at lock while still reffing the match – oom Toy told me this himself one evening in Pretoria.

Here in the Elgro, Basie Groenewald has just related how Polla Fourie, the former Springbok flanker, allegedly once asked the referee during a club match at Middelburg in the Transvaal to stop the game for a while. Old Polla then ran off the field to go and sort out someone in the crowd who had shouted a derogatory comment at him.

Basie Groenewald is talkative. 'The Blue Bulls and Griquas are my teams,' he says, and gestures towards the small blue plaster figure of a bull next to the Johnny Walker statuette on the counter.

This is something I often hear nowadays: on the platteland a guy will tell you: 'I support the Blue Bulls *and* Griquas.' Or: 'I support the Sharks *and* the Pumas.'

Once upon a time, when platteland rugby was still strong, they wouldn't have said that at all. They would simply have said: 'I support Griquas.'

'Ja-a-a,' old Basie sighs later. 'Rugby isn't the same any more.' It's as if the plattelanders' rugby loyalty is also moving to the cities these days.

And then Basie does something that any true Griquas supporter does frequently: 'How about it,' he asks, 'can you tell me all the names of the 1970 Griquas team?'

Without waiting for a response, Basie rattles off the names of that 1970 team as if reciting a magic formula with which he wants to call back a lost era.

Full back: Tos Smith

Wings: Buddy Swartz and Loekie van der Merwe

Centres: Mannetjies Roux and Koos Waldeck

Fly half: Piet Visagie

Scrum half: Joggie Viljoen

Eighth man: Dennys Vorster

Flanks: Piet van Deventer and Peet Smith

Locks: Jannie van Aswegen and Johan Scheepers

Hooker: James Combrinck

Props: Soon Nel and Popeye Joubert.

Over the years this team has become a symbol of what platteland rugby can achieve. Nearly all the players came from small towns: De Aar, Victoria West, and especially the Ammosal mine near Postmasburg. They were a valiant lot who on 18 September 1970 defeated the mighty Northern Transvaal – packed with defence force, police and Tukkies players – with a score of 11–9 at the De Beers stadium in Kimberley to win the Currie Cup.

Basie and other guys in these parts still talk about this victory as if it had happened yesterday.

I drive deeper into the interior, in the direction of Kuruman, because the town is reported to have a team again for the first time in years. And this is indeed so, I hear from an oom at the Engen filling station in the town. What's more, this team will be playing against Kathu's second team this evening. In Kathu.

Nico van der Westhuizen, chairman of the Kuruman rugby club, is someone who's working hard to get platteland rugby back on track. Last year he was part of a delegation who went to see Brian van Rooyen, president of SA Rugby.

Van Rooyen supposedly had all sorts of plans for platteland rugby. A Springbok amateur team, which would include platteland players in particular, would be selected. Platteland clubs would also receive more money.

But now everything is shrouded in uncertainty again. Van Rooyen has in the meantime been replaced by Oregon Hoskins, and Hoskins has not yet revealed his plans for platteland rugby.

To prevent teams from withdrawing shortly before a match, or simply not turning up, Nico and his fellow office-bearers have introduced a rule here: a team is fined R5 000 if it is responsible for a match not taking place. Dingleton, one of the other teams in the league, recently turned up at a match with only eleven players, but play they did.

The sun has already dipped behind Kathu's thorn trees when I arrive at the rugby field. It belongs to the Kathu mine and is in excellent condition.

The clubhouse is behind the posts, and as one enters it, memories of so many similar clubhouses return: the smell of Cobra polish, the wooden counter next to the wall, the straight row of chairs all along the wall, the trophies on the shelves, the team photographs on the walls.

On one side is a photograph in a special glass case: that Griquas team of 1970. There are also photographs of the Griquas players this club has produced: Stompie Nel, Boeta Wessels, Viervoet Liebenberg.

'Why is his nickname Viervoet?' I ask Hugo Schreuder, chairman of the Kathu Rugby Club.

'Because he was so tall.'

If his height was the issue, shouldn't he rather have been called Sewevoet Liebenberg? But platteland rugby nicknames often don't make sense: Boerram Venter, Papie Smit, Sailor Papenfus, Kierie Barnard.

John April, a deputy president of the Griquas Rugby Union, is also present. They're working hard here to keep rugby going, he says, but money remains a problem.

In the heyday of platteland rugby, guys sometimes turned out for the town team until late into their thirties. The fit and the less fit, the old and the young, all played together. It wasn't even unusual to hear a concerned son call out to his father in the scrum: 'Pa, are you orraait?'

But the youngsters who have run onto the field here in Kathu have all just recently left school. Not that they're scared of putting their bodies on the line: Jan Bester, Kathu's coach, has just complained that he bought more than three thousand rand's worth of Elastoplast for his players this year, and the stocks have almost run out again.

Seated on the pavilion are two hundred and thirty six people, plus a baby, a Maltese in a little red jersey, and Kuruman's seven reserves. One of the reserves, Johan Kruger, takes a relaxed draw on a Camel Ultimate Light. A number of spectators are standing on either side of the field.

Or, no, they're not standing: they're following the game up and down along the touchline in small flocks. Sometimes, when the battle heats up, they even venture a few steps onto the field itself, until the linesman chases them back to the touchline.

For a moment it almost feels as if the intensity of platteland rugby is making a comeback here in Kathu, especially when a fight breaks out among the players and a voice shouts from the crowd: 'Schoeman, you pig!'

A spectator next to the field has just labelled one of his team's wingers as *lazy*. 'He's not looking for work.'

This is a constant theme in platteland rugby: each team has at least one *lazy* winger. How come it's always a wing who's lazy, never a full back or a centre or a prop?

A platteland rugby team worth its salt always has the oddest code words for moves and throw-ins at the line-out: 'Pamela Anderson'. Or: 'Richelieu and Coke.' Also: 'Axes'.

A line-out is taking place. Kathu's throw-in. 'Peanut!' shouts Kathu's hooker, and holds the ball above his head.

'Peanut!' the scrum half screams to the fly half, who in turn shouts from behind his hand to the far-off winger: 'PEANUT!'

Just in case, one of the reserves next to the field also screams: 'PEANUT!'

Then the hooker throws in the ball right at the front on top of the props but, oh dear, unfortunately Kuruman steals the ball, while someone in the crowd shouts again: 'Schoeman, you pig!' In the end, Kuruman wins the game: 23–17.

Then Kathu's first team plays against Ammosal. The once mighty Ammosal, who contributed ten men to that 1970 Griquas team, loses 3–27 under the full moon that hangs above the stadium like a sorrowful eye.

Entering the Ammosal club building at Beeshoek, some 10 km outside Postmasburg, feels a bit like visiting a museum. First you walk through an entrance hall, and then you're in a small hall with wooden floors, a high ceiling and heavy velvet curtains. There are photographs on the wall of every team that has played for Ammosdal since the early 1950s.

You wonder how many rugby receptions have been held here over the decades. Do they still remember? There always used to be tiny frikadelletjies and cocktail sausages on toothpicks and solemn speeches in which Doc Craven was often thanked in his absence 'for everything he's doing for our rugby'.

Sometimes there was dancing, but by the end of the evening most of the men would be crowded together in the bar, reliving that try late in the second half, while the women would be sitting rather grumpily on chairs along the walls of the hall.

Pieter Wolmarans, the club manager, walks to the board on which the names of all the Ammosal Griquas players appear – and there they all are: Piet and Gawie Visagie, Joggie Viljoen, Gert Schutte, Kriek Erasmus, Jimmy Young.

But after 1993, not a single name. This was when things started going downhill for platteland rugby.

Another cause of the decline of platteland rugby, says Pietie Mostert, a former Griquas scrum half, is the disappearance of the smaller provincial unions. Young guys on the platteland stop playing earlier nowadays because there's no provincial team to aim for.

It used to be different: in the past you could play for North-Eastern Cape, North-Western Cape, Lowveld, Northern Natal, Far North, Eastern Free State, Stellaland, Vaal Triangle.

A man with scrum ears enters the bar next to the hall. 'Jis-jis, Jimmy,' he is greeted by some of the guys at the counter.

It's Jimmy Young, another Ammosal legend.

Here on the wall, hangs a framed report from the *Daily Mail* with a photo of a young Jimmy next to it. It was in 1976 that he was sent off the field in Kimberley by the referee, Professor Tinkie Heyns (does anyone still remember him, with his big shorts?). Griquas were playing against Andy Leslie's touring All Blacks team, and Jimmy had punched their lock, Frank Oliver, 'lights out'.

'Andy Leslie had hit me earlier in the game,' recalls oom Jimmy when asked about the incident. 'Then one of my guys kicked the ball high, and I rushed up, and then Oliver got in my way ...'

The old rugby stories are kept alive in bars like this. Some time ago, Piet Visagie, who now lives in Potchefstroom, had come to collect one of his Springbok jerseys, but he brought it back recently. It's more fitting, he felt, that it should hang here at Ammosal.

In one corner is an empty stool, with a sign above it: 'Jumbo's Corner'.

This is where Jumbo Harris, a cantankerous English gentleman who was also the mine manager, used to sit. Mister Harris, as everyone called him, was probably more responsible than anyone else for Griquas and Ammosal having once been such a powerful rugby force.

Mister Harris lured players to the mine and motivated them to play rugby, sometimes in a rather unorthodox way. Once, during a match, he shouted from the pavilion to Ammosal player Brinkie Combrinck: 'Combrinck, you're fired, you bastard!' But a few days afterwards he reappointed him at the mine.

Jimmy wants to show me something. We go outside to the rugby field. Famous teams came here to play: Tukkies, Maties, Pretoria
Police. He points to the western goal area. 'That's where we scat-
tered Mister Harris's ashes.'

We walk back. 'Maybe the field will be dug up one day,' says Jimmy. 'They say there's a lot of iron ore in the soil.'

In Daniëlskuil – approximately 70 km from Postmasburg, and one
of the towns of my youth – it's the same story: the pavilion's paint
is peeling and the grass on the field is knee high.

It was here that I saw my very first platteland match, at the age
of about eight or nine. I don't remember the players' names – none
of them played for Griquas. The only person who could be considered a rugby personality in Daniëlskuil in those days was tant Coenie Bredenkamp, the organist of the Dutch Reformed congregation.
She was the sister of the legendary radio commentator, Gerhard
Viviers, who was also known as 'Spiekeries'.

I sit down at the old pavilion, and remember: the sound of alu-
minium studs on a cement floor, an eighth man wearing a sweat-
band, Olympic boots with those square points, the red cord of a
referee's whistle, the smell of cinnamon sugar, a Ford 20 M on the
touchline sounding its hooter, a knee guard that has sagged right
down to a calf, someone shouting from this same pavilion: 'Get him!
Kill him!'

After all is said and done, this is perhaps all you can do: try to
remember everything you can about platteland rugby, and accept
that things will never be the same again.

Or go and watch one more platteland game, and hope that you
will be surprised.

I'm now on my way to Deben, a tiny village about 200 km north
of here, where the local guys are playing against Olifantshoek this
afternoon.

There are already about twenty cars parked around the field. The
first Deben player, with a blue knee guard, has just got out of a Nis-

san 1400 bakkie and lit a cigarette. Now he's quietly surveying the field, like a general forging battle plans.

It's a neat new field that has been laid out in the local township with the help of a Lotto grant. Olifantshoek is the odds-on favourite to win the match, because this is the first year Deben's had a rugby team after many years without one.

The team don't even have their own jerseys yet, and play in ones lent to them by Ammosal. The players arrive singly or in twos and threes, in a Cressida, an ageing Audi, a Hilux with a braai drum on the back, and a wheezy Nissan Stanza.

The moment Neels le Roux, Deben's coach, gets out of the bakkie, he begins to gather his troops: 'Come, boytjies! Come, come, come!'

A man in denim shorts, wearing a pair of rugby socks with his velskoene, has just arrived. This dress code is something you often see at a good platteland rugby game. Guys in the crowd wear rugby socks from their own playing days, and wiry ooms are attired in old club blazers with sleeves that are often too short. Just such an oompie, in a De Aar blazer, has taken up his seat in the front row of the pavilion.

Dirk Esterhuizen, a Deben supporter, puts up his hand to test the wind and says to a neighbour: 'I'm telling you, we must use the wind today.'

The wind is an important factor – and sometimes excuse – in such games, even if it's only a slight breeze, like the one stirring faintly over the field from the north.

Deben's players are now going into a huddle for the team talk. I move closer to them and when I hear what Neels is telling the guys, I know that the spirit of platteland rugby is still alive and well here.

'We must play open rugby today, boys,' says Neels, while the team forms a tight laager around him on the field. 'The chances are good that we're getting our jerseys next month, so remember, you're playing for a place in the team. You're playing for that jersey.'

He keeps quiet for a moment, to bring the message home to them.

Then he says to JP Greeff, the eighth man: 'Okay, captain, talk to them.'

JP addresses the team, in much stronger language. 'Listen up, boytjies,' he tells them. 'This is not a game for moffies. This is a shit-hard game. Aggressiveness hurts no one – except the other guys. Get bedonnerd, by all means. But channel your shit in the right way.

'If we can use all our aggression in the scrums, and if a back-line guy can take that ball and he breaks, oh, man, there's nothing sweeter than that. Believe me, it makes a forward's heart really happy when he sees that. I –'

'Captain,' interrupts a player wearing white boots. 'Tell them how important first-time tackling is.'

JP nods. 'Boys,' he says, 'it's vital: first-time tackling, first-time tackling, first-time tackling. You all know this –'

Another player interrupts JP. 'Also remember, boys,' he says, 'we don't try any fancy moves. We just play the game.'

In the Olifantshoek huddle there is less talking. 'I don't want any moaning on the field, okay?' the coach, Elré Miller, has just told them. 'This ref is a youngster. You can all see it. Don't piss him off. He could get hardegat. Just play the game.'

The players enter the smallish change rooms, and then comes one of the most important rituals of a platteland match: The Anointing of the Muscles with Deep Heat.

Ah, Deep Heat, the miracle cure-all. The ointment squeezed from this red-and-white tube is always rubbed in as if it's able to do far more than just soothe muscular aches. It is applied as an antidote to unfitness, deficient coaching, and even lack of talent.

Then, just before Deben runs onto the field, JP prays for the team: 'Dear Father, thank you for the opportunity we today have to demonstrate our talents to you. Be with each of the guys, so that we can achieve to the best of our ability. May there not be too many serious injuries. Be with us, and may the best team win. Amen.'

In a certain sense, the eighty minutes that the players spend on the field is not the most important part of platteland rugby.

It's about many other things: the town's involvement in the playing of the game, the bonding that happens in the huddle, the annual rugby dance and prize-giving ceremony, the stories that live on for years.

None of the team members receive a match fee. The rugby budget of Griquas – and many other smaller unions – is probably more modest than Percy Montgomery's shampoo sponsorship.

Within the first ten minutes, Olifantshoek scores the first try.

'Boys, come here,' calls JP, and gathers his troops behind the posts. 'They're heavier than us at the front. We can't take them on strength for strength. From now on we just play clever rugby. Boys, when you get the ball, put it over their heads so that they have to turn around. Crash-ball rugby will be of fuck-all use to us today. Clever rugby, boys. Clever rugby!'

But clever rugby has challenges of its own. Four minutes later, Olifantshoek scores another try.

JP assembles his troops again. 'What's going on, boys?' he asks. 'We're lying down! We must fight back!'

'First-time tackling, boys,' one of the other players reminds the men. 'First-time tackling!'

Olifantshoek scores yet another try. Next to the field Dirk Esterhuizen, the Deben supporter, anxiously asks the linesman: 'How long before half-time, Meneer?'

The linesman checks his watch. 'Eight minutes.'

'In the second half we're going to use that wind, hey,' says Dirk to the guy next to him.

Maybe a slight breeze against the shoulder blades really does help, because Deben does better in the second half. It takes Olifantshoek about fifteen minutes to score a try. Then another one follows. The score is now somewhere in the 30s to 0.

JP gathers his men again. 'Boys,' he says, 'as far as I'm concerned the score is still 0–0.'

'That goes for all of us,' says another player.

'First-time tackling, boys!' shouts someone. 'First-time tackling!'

Deben kicks off, wins a ruck soon afterwards, and there goes JP with the ball. It's as if Deben has suddenly been infused with the spirit of Mannetjies Roux and Tos Smith and Soon Nel and the rest of the 1970 Griquas. They maul the ball close to the try line and then JP again tries to break through. But he is stopped. 'Boys', he tells his guys a while later, 'I saw their try line right in front of me.'

All of a sudden it's as if these two teams are no longer just playing against each other. They're also playing for the smell of Deep Heat and the right to have a smoke before a game. They're playing for the right of mongrels to run onto the field, and of guys to blow the hooters of their cars. They're playing for friendship and rugby dances in the town hall and the spirit of Doc Craven and Jumbo Harris and the right to enjoy rugby without six-figure salaries, sponsored cars, sponsored sunglasses, sponsored golf clubs and sponsored cellphones.

They're playing for the damn survival of platteland rugby.

In the end, Olifantshoek wins the game 47–0.

'I'm proud of my men,' says Neels as his players leave the field. 'I'm very proud of them.'

The players form one big, collective circle on the field. Some spectators also come and join them. Others are already on their way to Die Doringdraad, the only bar in town, and Deben Rugby Club's unofficial clubhouse.

JP thanks the guys from Olifantshoek. Then Elré Miller also gets an opportunity to speak: 'Thanks very much for the spirit in which you played, boys. Good luck on the road ahead. You've got guts. Don't be disheartened, boys. We were also thrashed in the beginning, but we didn't chicken out. I'm just glad you're playing rugby, and not boozing and watching blue movies.'

The guys grip each other tighter, and one shouts: 'Rugby!'

Then the others answer: 'Rugby, yeah!'

On the straight and narrow through Bushmanland

Oom Koos Louw sits in his house next to the old-age home in Pofadder and taps his fingers together thoughtfully.

'Let me tell you something about Pofadder you don't yet know,' he says as he fixes his gaze on me.

I know that Pofadder was named after Klaas Pofadder, leader of a Koranna community that lived in the Northern Cape in the 1800s.

Pofadder is also the unofficial capital of Bushmanland. It has three cafés, two filling stations, a Spar, an orphanage, and a lekker hotel with a parrot called Vicegrip that sits in a cage in the lobby. Besides all this, the bar has two goldfish in a tank and an electronic dartboard that automatically registers your score.

Recently, Pofadder also got a new China shop, with a couple behind the counter who speak only Mandarin, which means there are probably more Mandarin speakers in the town than there are English speakers.

What else does one need to know about Pofadder?

'The longest straight stretch of road in South Africa lies between here and Kliprand,' he says, letting the cat out of the bag.

Oom Koos, who has just turned eighty, ought to know, because he was once a Member of the Provincial Council for this area. He knows the roads around here like he knows the veins on the back of his hand. He grew up here, and is writing a book on the region.

I check my road map. Indeed: the R358 from Pofadder to Kliprand, to the south-west, stretches over more than 200 km. And the road is very, very straight. Yet even so, it does make the odd little bend.

Are the straight bits between those kinks longer than, for instance, the dead-straight 54 km between Olifantshoek and Upington? Some people say *that* is the longest straight stretch of road in the country.

And what about that stretch between Bothaville and Hoopstad in the Free State, which is surely also longer than 50 km?

'Measure it yourself,' oom Koos says. 'Just go and measure it.'

It's a good idea. I've been here for more than a day, and I've spent so much time in the hotel that I'm worried that Vicegrip will start using my first name when I next walk past him in the lobby. I'm keen to discover Bushmanland.

I could do a 4x4 route, or tear around on a quad bike, or canoe down the Orange River. But frankly, I'd rather drive the R358.

That's because, like love and marriage, long roads and tall stories go together.

It's not a bad idea to hang around in Pofadder for a day or two if you want to set off to explore Bushmanland. The town is small, but there are plenty of good places to stay.

It can also help to ease you into a slower, more relaxed rhythm.

Perhaps it's the influence of this empty, quiet, timeless landscape that makes it feel as if things happen more slowly here. The people drive slowly, they walk slowly. It even looks as if those two goldfish in the bar swim more slowly than others.

And people talk slowly.

'My . . . boy,' a man at the filling station said to me this morning. 'The . . . first . . . time . . . a . . . car . . . came . . . through . . . this . . . area . . . the . . . people . . . fetched . . . cardboard . . . boxes . . . and . . . covered . . . the . . . tracks . . . so . . . that . . . the . . . wind . . . wouldn't . . . blow . . . them . . . away . . . before . . . other . . . people . . . had . . . a . . . chance . . . to see . . . them.'

Besides, if you just zoom by in your car, as many people do, you'll miss all the interesting plants and flowers in the veld: the vygies, calendulas, sporries, gazanias. You'll also miss out on the herby smells that the drab bossies give off in the evening as the hot sun begins to set.

And if you try to rush people around here, you'll miss out on all the local expressions and stories. And you won't have time to go and have a Moerse Burger – yes, it's called a Moerse Burger. That's what it says on the menu at the Bushmanland café.

I came straight to this café in the main road after my chat with oom Koos Louw, and ordered a burger for R18,95 (chips not included). Now I'm waiting, because things don't run on McDonald's time here in this café.

In the meantime, Floors Cloete, who has also stopped at the café, clears up another question that has been bothering me: where are Bushmanland's actual borders?

'Bushmanland doesn't actually have borders, my friend,' he says. 'It lies here in the north-west, around Pofadder and the Orange River. Everybody has their own borders. The way I look at it, if it's grassland, then it's Bushmanland. When it turns to scrubland, then you're in Namaqualand.'

And then my Moerse Burger arrives. Like a young tortoise, it squats in the styrofoam container with a lonely bit of lettuce, a slice of cucumber and a piece of tomato as a garnish. Just the thing for tackling the R358 from here to Kliprand, because, according to the map, there are no towns between here and there.

I sit in the car and eat outside the café. You can taste the meaty flavour of Bushmanland in the burger. I only manage half, and then I'm full, and give the rest to a beggar called Captain.

I set the trip meter to zero, point the Condor's nose southwards, and head out of town on the Kliprand road past the clinic, trailing a small cloud of dust behind me

In the *Guinness Book of Records* there is no entry for long, straight roads. But on the Internet I was able to establish that the 234 km span between Hickson and Streeter in North Dakota is the longest straight stretch of road in the United States, and in Australia it's the 148 km stretch on the Eyre highway between Perth and Adelaide. We'll have to see if the R358 can beat that.

The road is a bit rough at the start, but I get up to 80 km/h on the open road. After exactly 13,8 km, I stop. Around me there are just wide, open plains.

For a moment, I consider triumphantly punching the air with my fist because I've just broken a record: New Zealand might be able to beat us at rugby and netball, but we've beaten them on this one. Their longest straight stretch of road is 13,7 km, near the town of Culverden on South Island.

I get back in and drive on, but after about 15 km of straight road, a few ridges rise above the plain. And then the road makes a slight kink as it finds its way through them. Oh dear, I'll have to reset the trip meter to zero again.

Now the road is taking several turns. On the left is a signboard for a farm: *Witkoppies*. I take the turn-off. Maybe somebody around here can tell me where those really long straight bits of road are.

The Witkoppies farmyard is a typical Bushmanland farmyard: first you see the windmill, then the cement dam, and then the sheep kraal. Prickly pear cactus grows here, and near the wide stoep of the farmhouse is an old bakkie with railings on the back for transporting sheep. I also notice a rain gauge on a pole. (There are in fact eight rain gauges on Witkoppies, I would discover.)

As I pull up outside the house, a deeply tanned man comes through the small silver gate that is the entrance to the bare front yard. Behind him trails a small dog.

Piet Truter and Kambro.

No, no, says Piet. The really, really straight, long stretches of road are further on down the R358. 'But, first, come in for a bit!'

I'm not going to be able to make a quick escape, I realise, because there are few people as hospitable as the Bushmanlanders. We head for the back door, and I notice all sorts of things that are no longer seen in farmyards around South Africa today.

In front of the step at the back stoep is a car's radiator for wiping your feet on before you enter the house. This makeshift doormat used to be a common sight at the back door of farmhouses.

Piet opens the creaking screen door – these aren't that common today either – and we step into a Cobra-polished corridor. In the lounge is a display cabinet filled with teaspoons, small three-legged pots and other ornaments, and on top is the graduation photograph of one of the younger members of the household.

It's the next morning, and I'm back in Pofadder because things turned out just as I'd expected: I got stuck with Piet Truter at Witkoppies and had to go back to the hotel for the night before attempting the road again. (Vicegrip didn't remember my name, though.)

Piet made me get into his Nissan bakkie, and he and Kambro and I drove to the open plains of Witkoppies. Piet knows every bush, plant and grass by name. We stopped at many of them and he introduced them to me as if they were old friends.

He has identified more than a hundred and fifty plant species around here.

It's been a good year for Bushmanland. The average annual rainfall is just over 100 mm, but this year they had more than 300 mm. As Piet says: 'This is a grateful part of the world. If it rains, the veld quickly turns beautiful.'

When it doesn't rain, however, it becomes a cruel world. Boreholes and wells dry up. Animals and plants die. Everything gets drier and dustier (and slower).

'That's when you get depressed,' says Piet. 'That's when you get depressed.'

Like the farmer last night who told the story about a recurring dream he'd had during a drought: he's in his lounge and there's a knock at the front door. And every time he opens the door it's one of his sheep that has come to say goodbye.

The old trekboers . . . you can't help thinking about them when you drive this road. They were the toughest of the tough.

Piet Truter and many of the farmers in this region are descendants of the original trekboers who moved here in the late 1800s from the Cape. The Bushmanland voortrekkers is what some called them. They weren't all white. There were also coloured people and so-called 'basters'. And they experienced just about as much hardship and grief as did the Voortrekkers who left the Cape for the Transvaal and Natal in 1838.

On the seat next to me is a book called *Pioniers van die Dorsland*, by PJ van der Merwe. The author was a professor of history at Stellenbosch University who travelled through this region in the 1940s and talked to many of the original trekboers. 'Every time I go to the north-west,' he wrote, 'I feel as if I'm a traveller going to discover a new country.'

It's a bit how I feel when I look at the trip meter clocking up the kilometres as I drive: 24 km, 25 km . . . This is the distance of straight road the R358 has delivered up since I reset it to zero just past the farm Houmoed.

You don't see many farmsteads. It's just this flat bit of earth, with the straight road that lies ahead: 26 km, 27 km . . .

One thing is immediately evident: almost all the signboards are full of bullet holes. What's going on in the mind of a person who shoots holes in road signs? Are they alone when they do it? Or do some ordinary family men get so bored driving this long, straight bit of road through this empty world that they feel driven to reach for the nine mil under the Camry's seat to shoot holes in the road signs, while the wife asks anxiously: 'What are you doing, sweetie?'

32 km, 33 km . . .

And then, dammit, the road makes another kink, presumably to avoid that little vlei over there.

I stop and reset the trip meter to zero again.

About 5 km on, between nothing and nowhere but still on the R358, I come across a man standing next to a bakkie on the road. I stop.

He's wearing an overall, and he's been screwing his eyes against the Bushmanland sun for so long now that they're permanent slits.

Gideon is his name – Gideon Titus. He's a fencer by profession.

''n Skaap is maar 'n anner affêring,' he says. 'Hy kan met 'n draad tekere gaan lat dit 'n arrigheid is.' (A sheep is something else. It can go crazy and damage a fence like nobody's business.)

Like many others around here, Gideon is a poet without being aware of it. He talks about '*douspoor*' (early in the morning), '*fyn van vel*' (sensitive), and '*swerfklippe*' (stones that lie in a heap in the veld as if they've sought one another out for company over the centuries).

Gideon had also known Piet van den Heever, a Bushmanland farmer I visited a few years ago, who shared his stories with me.

We lean back against Gideon's bakkie and reminisce about oom Piet for a while.

Oom Piet's forebears were trekboers. There were few people who could tell a story the way he did. He claimed that he once killed a leopard (or a *tier,* as the people around here call it) with a car jack after he caught it in a trap.

'I went to set the trap,' he said. 'And the next morning we drove past, me and old Gert, a man who was on pension. We stopped at the trap, and I saw, ja, there was the leopard.

'It was crouching. And it was angry. Its beard was flapping around. Old Gert closed the bakkie's window, but I said: 'Open it, man. I want to see what's going on.

'And old Gert opened the window and pointed to the leopard with his finger. Don't ever do that, *ever*. The leopard pulled in its neck and growled even more fiercely.

'I asked old Gert: "Where's the jack?"

' "Behind the backrest," said Gert.

'I said: "Give it to me."

'Man, and then I climbed out of the bakkie and with the jack in my hand I walked and stood where I could look the leopard in the eye. And I took that jack and I knocked it over the head. Dead.'

This a cruel world, yes – for both animal and man.

Oom Piet died on his farm at Koenabib near Pofadder a few years ago after he was seriously assaulted with a blunt object.

The area around the R358 south of Pofadder is rather flat, but people call this 'the hill'. 'We live on the hill,' they would say. Or: 'There's been good rain on the hill.'

It's because this area is quite a bit higher above sea level than the part of Bushmanland that lies to the north of Pofadder.

I say goodbye to Gideon Titus and drive on, while the trip meter continues to measure the next straight stretch of road on the R358: 28 km, 29 km . . .

I notice a sign next to the road: Kliprand 0.

Actually, it's still 120 km to Kliprand, but someone has scratched out the 1 and the 2. Bored farm kids?

Here and there, you see a windmill next to the road. In one spot, in a radius of about 50 m, there are six windmills. Almost everything in this part of the world is determined by the availability – or absence – of water.

The old trekboers moved around freely, and wherever they found water they would make camp and sometimes stay for months. They let their animals graze in the veld, and they hunted – especially springbok.

'As far as the eye could see, the herds of cattle grazed,' writes Professor Van der Merwe in his book.

'Around each vlei a city of tents arose. At each tent there would be poles from which hung a hundred pounds of wet biltong. Hunting was forbidden, but nobody took any notice.

73

'Nollie Townshend, a police officer and game ranger, was stationed at Okiep. As soon as he set out from the town, people would make a fire to send a smoke signal. The farmers would see the smoke and make fires to warn others of his approach.'

Eventually, Townshend got help, and the laws of the Cape were applied more strictly in this area.

In 1908, two land surveyors, Engelbert Krapohl and Johann Leipoldt, began the job of surveying Bushmanland. In due course the area was divided into farms, and the farmers had to buy their land from the government.

The farm Consentvlei was one of the last to be surveyed and sold, according to Professor Van der Merwe. That was in 1926. I've just stopped at the sign to Consentvlei on the R358. It's about 30 km after the last kink in the road.

It can get lonely on the R358, because there's not even cellphone reception here. I drive on, but again there's a little turn in the road. Oh, man! And then there's a turn-off to the right. It goes to Gamoep and Bosluispan, and a few other places.

I look around: there's not a sign of another person anywhere. Maybe I should go to Bosluispan. The place has a story – a rather sad one.

I turn off. About 10 km from the R358, on the road to Gamoep, there's a huge pan in the middle of the plain. Bosluispan.

It was here, more than fifty years ago, where a proud people first lived: the Bosluis Basters – as, to this day, they describe themselves. Finding the exact place won't be easy, though, as there aren't any signboards.

Fortunately, I have Barry Eksteen's *BBs van die Boesmanland* with me. In his book, Eksteen gives directions to the farm Bosluis, which lies near the pan, the place where the Bosluis Basters once lived.

They were no different from the other trekboers from the Cape, except that they were classified 'coloured', so they weren't allowed to own land.

Over time, they came together at this farm called Bosluis next to the pan. The reason? Hannes Meyer, the white farm owner, had a relationship with a coloured woman. Oom Hannes looked beyond skin colour. That's why they were allowed to live on his farm.

But the farm wasn't big enough for everyone to farm on it.

So where could they go? Where would they find a home?

A missionary from Pofadder, Dominee Pieter Eksteen, began ministering to their spiritual needs. He also got involved in the search for a permanent place that would be big enough for them to live and farm.

Just before the pan, I turn right down a road that winds round its edge. A tumbleweed is being blown along by the hot wind. A rusty wreck of a Chev El Camino lies in the middle of the pan – or perhaps it's a Ford Ranchero.

It feels as if you're driving into a quiet space within yourself when you drive alongside this pan, with dead silence outside, and mirages hovering all around you.

The pan is about 25 km long and 6 km wide. Near the northernmost point the road turns sharply right and runs across the pan. All around lie piles of soil. Somebody once tried to find diamonds here – and found a few, perhaps.

But where are the diamond diggers now? Who knows? There are just a few corrugated iron buildings, a tractor and a front-end loader.

A little further on, on the opposite side of the pan, is the ruin of a house. Across from it is the rubble of another building. This was once the home of Hannes Meyer, owner of the farm Bosluis.

I stop and get out. Flies buzz around my head.

In this little house, Hannes Meyer had to make a serious decision one night: he had to decide whether to remain 'white'.

In 1949, Dominee Eksteen secured a large piece of land for the Bosluis Basters from the government, in the Richtersveld, about 300 km from here. The Bosluis people would have to move there, but if Hannes wanted to move with his wife Sophie, he would have to have himself classified 'coloured'. (The Population Registration Act was promulgated a year later.) A government official arrived at his door one day and put the choice to him.

I head towards the house. The door is open. Thick dust lies everywhere. In the corner, wasps are building a nest.

What did Hannes say to the official on that day? How did he react when he heard that he would have to choose what race he wanted to be, white or coloured? Did he walk out of the door and go and sit on a rock, light his pipe and stare quietly across the plains? Or did he cry with rage across the emptiness?

The most important thing is that oom Hannes chose love. He allowed himself to be reclassified 'coloured' and went along with the rest of the people to the Richtersveld, where he later died and was buried.

I walk back to my car and drive back slowly to the R358.

Every deserted house has its story.

I am back on the R358 and drive up to a slight bend in the road on the farm Stofvlei. It's about 85 km to Kliprand. Once again, the road lies as straight as a knitting needle ahead of me.

I set the trip meter to zero for the nth time.

The road is not too bad at this point, but I'm still sticking to 80 km/h. You don't want to have any mishaps here. Since leaving Pofadder this morning, I've seen only Gideon Titus, the fencer, on the road.

As I approach Kliprand, the land becomes more uneven. Everywhere there are ridges and dips.

Centuries ago, geologists claim, there was an ancient river called the Koa, which ran from south to north through Bushmanland in the direction of Goodhouse at the Orange River.

Beyond the farm Tiervlei, it looks as if I've finally found the longest straight stretch of road in the country, because now the trip meter shows 50 km – and the road ahead points to the horizon like an index finger.

50 km . . . 52 km . . . 53 km . . ..

Then I see a bakkie next to the road with two men nearby. One has a large contraption on his back, and a pipe in his hand.

It's Piet van der Westhuizen and Dries Visser, and they are spraying locusts. I stop next to them.

'They eat everything in sight,' says Piet, pointing to the right and left. 'Just look how many there are.'

It looks as if the earth is trembling, but if you look carefully you see thousands of locusts jumping. Piet runs off to one side, with the nozzle like a machine gun in his hand. He sprays the poison left and right.

It looks as if the sprayers are winning the battle, because later they take time to have a long chat with me.

There are people whose cars overturn here from time to time, they say. One Christmas a few years ago, a petrol tanker overturned and it burst into flames.

'Two guys burnt to death,' Piet says. 'I saw the bodies myself.'

I say goodbye to Piet and Dries and aim for Kliprand, and the trip meter is still counting: 55 km, 56 km, 57 km . . . At 60 km, the road ahead of me is still dead straight.

Why this fascination with the longest straight road?

Maybe it's because today most of us are confined to life in the cooped-up spaces of cities. It's great to know there's open space out there where you can just drive, and drive, and drive.

Open spaces allow you to dream dreams of freedom.

The trip meter has just ticked over to 70 km. Oom Koos Louw is probably right: this must be the longest straight stretch of road in the country.

It keeps going: 75 km, 77 km . . .

Then, a bit further on, there's a big, green signboard indicating a road to the left: *Platbakkies*. Not far from this I see a twist in the road.

I stop just before the turn: 79,3 km, says the trip meter.

At first, it's something of an anticlimax. It feels as if there should have been a ribbon to mark the imaginary finish line. Maybe there ought to have been a girl next to the road with one of those big bottles of champagne that Formula One racing drivers spray all over one another and the front-row spectators.

But it's just me and this road.

I get out.

'We drive far too quickly nowadays,' writes Professor Van der Merwe in his book. 'The car has spoilt us. Because the car doesn't get tired, people don't have to stop and rest. The result is that people race from hotel to hotel and don't stop to talk to anyone along the way. If you drive like this, you see nothing.'

I stand there for a long time, looking across the open plains. And then it hits me: the silence. Bliss.

This is how a long, straight stretch of road rewards you.

Trans-Karoo-o-oo . . .

The train should have left already. Oom Willie is getting agitated. He taps impatiently on his watch. Half past ten has come and gone.

'We're running six minutes late,' he says, and peers out of the window. 'In my day, this wouldn't have happened. We used to run things to the minute!'

It's a Tuesday morning, and oom Willie Crause and I are standing in the corridor of a passenger coach at a platform at Johannesburg station. Both of us are bound for Cape Town. He and his wife, Mara, are going to visit their daughter in Durbanville. And I want to experience once again what it's like to travel by train.

I want to find out whether travelling by train is the same as it was in the days before Greyhound buses and cheap air tickets. Is it still safe on the train? Do they still serve three-course meals in the dining car in the evening? Who in South Africa still takes the train?

Oom Willie and his wife are two compartments down the corridor from my own. He is a retired station foreman, but is still entitled to an annual free pass to any place in the country that can be reached by train.

I, too, have some railway experience: in 1984 I worked for two months as a waiter on this train between Johannesburg and Cape Town. Back then it was known as the Trans-Karoo, but nowadays it's called the Shosholoza Meyl ('meyl' is township slang for train).

The toilet at the end of the corridor is the same cramped, grey cubicle as in the past, down to the lingering smell of Dettol. Everything is neat and clean, and the compartments also look pretty much the same: there is still a wide seat with two sleeping berths above it, and in the corner there's still one of those mirrors that distort your face so badly that you look like you've got a serious case of mumps.

But there's one thing missing: those cushions shaped like a sausage roll that used to lie on the seat. A camel turd, we called it.

How many of those cushions were tossed out of train windows by drunk army conscripts, students or school children over the years? Just for fun.

In the days when he was still in the employ of the then South African Railways and Harbours (SAR & H), says oom Willie, the driver of this train would have had to complete a delay report, because we should have departed at half past ten.

In her book *Ysterwiele*, where she records the stories of railway workers of yore, Werna Maritz tells of an Afrikaans-speaking train driver who had to write such a report in English: 'When about to start with my train at 12h30, I received an unforeseen, urgent call of nature,' the driver explained. 'I went to the nearest convenience situated on platform 1 at Cape Town station. While relieving myself, I felt so satisfied that I almost forgot that there was such an institution as the SAR & H.'

Transnet, as the old SAR & H is now known, hasn't completely forgotten about us, because just after twenty to eleven a whistle blows somewhere, and a few seconds later we start moving.

It's as if I suddenly hear a familiar voice from the past: tickety-tick, tickety-tick . . .

The compartment to my left is occupied by three ladies from

Roodepoort. They are members of a bowls team on their way to a tournament in Cape Town. To my right is a couple from Zambia with a baby, as well as a bunch of wooden giraffes and other flea-market articles they obviously plan on hawking in Cape Town.

There's also a group of Dutch tourists on the train.

'Right away, ou maat,' says oom Willie as we begin to move. 'Right away.' It's the railway old-timers' version of 'Bon voyage'.

Why do trains have such an effect on the imagination? Just think of all the songs that have been written about trains, like the Radio Kalahari Orkes's 'Kaptein, Kaptein, Waarheen Ry die Trein?' or that old country number by George Hamilton IV that was so popular in South Africa in the 1980s, 'Blue Train'.

There have also been many train movies: *The Great Train Robbery*, *Doctor Zhivago*, *Murder on the Orient Express*, and the Hitchcock thriller *Strangers on a Train*.

And who still remembers Budd Spencer and Terence Hill, in the 1972 hit movie *Trinity is Still my Name*, riding across a Wild West plain in a steam locomotive while eating baked beans from a blackened pan? At the time we all yearned to escape to freedom on such a train, just like old Budd and Terence.

'The train offers the maximum of opportunity with the minimum of risk,' writes Paul Theroux, the famous American travel writer. 'A train journey is travel; everything else – planes especially – is transfer, your journey beginning when you arrive.'

We are now pulling slowly out of Johannesburg station and almost all the passengers are in their compartments, gazing out of the windows.

In a train it so often feels as if you're being hypnotised by the landscape outside. You just sit and stare and stare. Perhaps it's because you don't need to worry about the traffic or the right route. You can simply sit back and observe the world from a fresh, sideways angle while being gently lulled: tickety-tick, tickety-tick . . .

Johannesburg's station building has been refurbished and extended. But the Blue Room doesn't exist any more. Once upon a time, the Blue Room was among the classiest restaurants in Johannesburg. Families often used to go there for a three-course Sunday lunch.

At least the Benson & Hedges building is still there to the right, opposite the station. (It used to have an advert for Benson & Hedges on it, hence the name.)

That's the building where you used to go to apply for work on the railways. Many people can tell you stories about the Benson & Hedges building: how they spent a whole day, sometimes more than a day, being sent from pillar to post on different floors for interviews, to fill in forms, and to complete aptitude tests.

You also had to take a bilingualism test. 'Make a sentence with the word "hole",' was one question. 'I sit on my hole, sir,' was the answer one applicant apparently gave.

In 1989, before the start of the so-called rationalisation of the railways, the SAR & H had about twenty-five thousand employees. Today the number is much lower.

The Shosholoza Meyl no longer departs daily from Pretoria to Cape Town, as the Trans-Karoo used to do. Nowadays it leaves from Johannesburg, and only on Sundays, Tuesdays and Fridays. A tourist class ticket (that's the old first class) from Johannesburg to Cape Town costs R320.

We've barely left the station when there's a knock at the door of my compartment. I slide it open. It's a waiter in a bright purple shirt. 'Something to drink, sir?' he asks.

I point to the purple shirt. 'Don't you guys wear uniforms any more?'

'This is our uniform, sir.'

They're lucky. When I was a train waiter we had to wear those heavy blue uniforms, with a white shirt and tie. Boy, you used to sweat in that uniform, especially when the chief started barking his orders.

He was in charge of the dining car, but everyone knew him as the 'chief' and addressed him as such. He was usually a fierce old railway stalwart with years of experience, who ran the dining car like a sergeant major.

Every day we had to polish the Sheffield knives and forks, sweep the dining car, wash the tables. (Chief Swanepoel, our chief, had one important criterion for anything shiny: he wanted to see his face reflected in it so clearly that 'I'll be able to comb my hair'.)

Your day started early when you or one of your fellow waiters walked down the corridor with the ding-dong gong and woke the passengers. Then coffee was served to each compartment in turn.

The serving of the coffee was a time of somewhat nervous anticipation for us waiters because of rumours about lonely women trying to seduce waiters at that hour of the morning – a fate that, unfortunately, befell neither me nor any of my colleagues. (Although one did claim that a woman in a nightie had once given him a come-hither look.)

I make my way to the dining car, passing a compartment with two security guards in blue uniforms. These two, together with a number of other guards, are accompanying us to Cape Town to make sure that the passengers are safe.

Things have changed in the dining car.

The tables are no longer covered with starched white tablecloths, as in the past. There aren't any silver knives and forks, and the silver fruit bowl with real fruit is no longer on the sideboard.

Two waitresses in purple uniforms are chatting at a table. They're friendly and talkative. Women didn't work on trains in the old days.

'Where's the chief?' I ask.

They look mystified. 'Chief?' one asks. 'What's that?'

We've now left Johannesburg and have passed Potchefstroom and Klerksdorp, where the newlyweds Stephan and Annelie Schutte have boarded the train. They're on their way to Cape Town for the last leg of their honeymoon.

Oom Willie Crause joins me at my table in the dining car. We drink coffee from paper cups as the train passes slowly through Makwassie station without stopping.

Like many other towns in the country, Makwassie used to have a smart station that competed annually for the prestigious award of neatest station in the country.

Now the door frames and window frames of the main building are missing. It looks as if someone has made a fire in the signal room – the walls are covered with dark smoke stains. The row of red-brick station houses next to it are also in ruins. The gardens are overgrown, and it's been years since the red stoeps have had a decent layer of Sunbeam polish.

'It's tragic to see everything in this state,' says oom Willie, while the station slides past. 'It's a damn shame, isn't it?'

In the past few years, Transnet has already put about eight thousand railway houses and seven hundred and eighty-nine stations up for sale. At present there are also 2 434 km of railway line in the country that are no longer being maintained, the Minister of Transport, Jeff Radebe, told parliament recently.

'Let me tell you a story,' says oom Willie, as if he wants to cheer both of us up. 'In the 1920s, my late father's brother travelled by train for the first time from Cape Town to Beaufort West.'

Just outside Worcester, he apparently ordered coffee, and as he took his first sip, the train entered the tunnel through the Hex River mountains. All of a sudden it was pitch-dark in the compartment.

Deeply concerned, oom Willie's father's brother asked his fellow passenger: 'Ou swaer, have you drunk any of your coffee yet?'

'No,' he replied from the gloom.

'Don't touch it, ou swaer. I've just had some of mine and now I'm blind as a bat!'

It's already dark when we rumble into Kimberley station.

Kimberley is the home of arguably the most eccentric train enthusiast in the country: Dr Peter le Sueur. He has a doctorate in train engineering, and has travelled every railway line in South

Africa and sketched a floor plan of every station. He also knows by heart the timetable of every long-distance passenger train in the country.

Once, long ago, I bumped into Dr Le Sueur at Kimberley station. It was from him that I first heard about James Wide and his baboon, Jack – a story that railway old-timers tell each other over and over again in wonderment.

Wide, who worked as a conductor, lost both his legs in a train accident in the 1880s. He was then offered the job of signal master at Uitenhage station. But he sometimes found it difficult to work the signals. One day, Wide bought a young baboon from someone, and started teaching it how and when to pull the signals.

In the end, the story goes, Jack the baboon was for all practical purposes the signal master at Uitenhage. According to a newspaper article that appeared at the time, 'The intelligence of this animal was almost too strange to be credited.'

The Meyl only stops for about twenty minutes in Kimberley. I get out of the train to stretch my legs, but there's no sign of Dr Le Sueur. (Look out for him if you're ever at Kimberley station. He sometimes still hangs around there. It'd be worth your while to chat to him.)

A man comes walking along the platform. He's wearing a yellow reflective jacket and is carrying a hammer with a long handle.

It's Johan Meiring, a wheel tapper. Every time a train enters the station, he has to tap each wheel with his hammer. The sound it makes tells him whether or not it is cracked.

'It makes a faint, dull sound if it's cracked,' says Johan. 'You can hear it immediately.'

If a carriage has a cracked wheel, it is uncoupled straight away.

Johan has been working as a wheel tapper for more than twenty-five years. He was also once a callman.

In the old days, a callman played an important role on the railways. It was his job to wake up the train drivers, conductors and other staff at night so that they could start their shifts on time.

85

Back then, a callman would travel by bicycle and carry a little book that had to be signed by every person he woke. This was to prevent them from blaming him if they were late for work.

As far as he knows, this job doesn't exist any more, Johan says. Nowadays most of the drivers have cellphones.

We are now outside Kimberley, making our way through the dark night to De Aar via Witput and Hopetown. The first train travelled from the Cape to Kimberley as far back as the 1880s.

It's time for dinner, but, no, this train no longer offers elaborate three-course meals. Tonight the choice is between steak and, well, steak. With vegetables and potatoes on the side. And it's a very tasty meal.

Some distance beyond Kimberley, at Beaconsfield, the train comes to a halt in the darkness. The electric locomotives are now going to be uncoupled and replaced with diesel locomotives.

It's dead quiet outside, and then you hear it: the sound of a train shunting. Shunting takes place when carriages are uncoupled and hitched to other locomotives, an activity that is accompanied by loud, clanking noises.

Who doesn't know the awe-inspiring, nostalgic sound of shunting trains? Anyone who grew up near railway yards or on the platteland would be familiar with it: you are a child and asleep in your warm bed. Then, in the depths of the night, you are suddenly woken by the distant sounds of things bashing against each other, roaring engines and blowing whistles.

Your initial reaction is one of fear, but then you realise that you're safe. It's just the trains shunting at the station.

Oom Willie and I stand outside in the corridor and listen to the sounds as if it were music. When he worked on the railways, they still used steam locomotives. It's as if the shunting of the train has shaken loose all kinds of distant memories in his mind.

He talks about the steam locomotives as if they're old friends of his: the 16 E, the 26 class, the 32 class. . .

The radio station RSG used to broadcast a programme called *Op die Voetplaat* (On the Footplate) in the early hours of the morning. Drivers, stokers and other train people would phone in and tell their stories – stories of the hard times and the good times.

In this hot region a train driver – and a stoker, of course – had to be tough. Many of their names are still mentioned with respect among train people: Sidney van Biljon, Bok de Beer, Chris Beytell . . .

Men with rough hands who wore those special round caps and never boarded a locomotive without a brightly polished shift box. Some read the Bible and prayed before the start of a shift; others could be pretty grumpy and might snarl at a young stoker: 'Don't call me oom, I'm not your uncle, do you hear! I'm not married to your auntie! Call me sir or driver!'

But Transnet stopped using steam locomotives in the early 1980s. Nowadays they only get hauled out for short pleasure trips.

Once upon a time, there were more than a hundred train drivers stationed at De Aar. Today there are fewer than forty. After Germiston, it was the busiest station in the country.

It's almost eleven o'clock at night as we enter De Aar station. In the steam-train era conditions were different here. Even at this time of the night, the arrival of a train would have caused a flurry of activity on the platform. Porters would have pushed forward with their two-wheel trolleys, a relief driver would have stood up from a slatted bench where he was waiting, the lights would have been blazing in the restaurant, somewhere there would have been music playing, and at the row of tickey boxes a few passengers would have been making a last call.

Now the station is all but deserted. A couple of passengers are ambling towards the train.

There are no sounds of shunting trains, and the restaurant as well as the famous bar at De Aar closed down years ago. Only one of the town's four hotels is still operating.

More than a hundred train carriages were recently sold off here at a public auction – mainly to mining companies and big scrap-yards.

De Aar's fate is the same as that of many other towns where there used to be major railway junctions and yards. Noupoort, Co-ligny, Waterval-Boven and Touws River – they've all gone into de-cline since the government decided to privatise the railways in the late 1980s.

But the current government has new plans for De Aar. Deputy President Phumzile Mlambo-Ngcuka has announced a plan to pro-mote the transport of goods by rail, and to inject new life into De Aar. Many people around here are optimistic that the town will shake off its rust.

Who hasn't yet slept on a train? Is there a better place to sleep than on a train?

You still get a flimsy blanket, two sheets and a softish pillow, but, so what, there's a cool breeze flowing in from the window and outside the stars glide past, low and bright, while the wheels rock you to sleep with their tickety-tick, tickety-tick.

During the night I wake up. The train has stopped again. I hear voices outside and peer out of the window. We're at Hutchinson station, which was built in 1884.

A man and a woman embrace on the platform. Then the man boards the train, a suitcase in his hand.

For many people, trains also represent parting.

A cup of station coffee would have been welcome, but here as well, the station restaurant closed down long ago.

Station coffee didn't taste like other coffee. This is because it was made differently. Werna Maritz divulges the recipe in her book *Ysterwiele*. The following ingredients were required for lo-comotive-strong station coffee: one cup of coffee grounds, three cups of sugar, six cups of boiling water and one teaspoon of salt.

The sugar was melted to make a syrup, and then the coffee grounds were stirred in. Then came the boiling water and salt.

The train starts moving again. We're travelling deeper into the interior, past Nelspoort and Beaufort West. Near Laingsburg it starts getting light. I go outside into the corridor. A man comes past, dressed in a purple shirt like the waiter's. It's oom Dawie Breedt.

Oom Dawie is the conductor, nowadays known as a train manager. We talk as we look out of the window at the trucks passing us one after the other on the N1 that runs next to the railway line. In the days of steam locomotives, everyone's big fear was getting a piece of soot in the eye if you stuck your head out of the train window.

In a certain sense, those trucks are the reason why fewer and fewer people are transporting their goods by train.

But oom Dawie isn't pessimistic about the future of trains in South Africa. Many people still travel by train, he says. During the last December holidays, a large number of extra trains had to be arranged to provide for the additional passengers.

The station at Touwsrivier looks even more dilapidated than that at De Aar. Few trains still stop here. And to think that this was once a bustling railway town, with hundreds of railway houses.

Today, many of these old houses are sold for exorbitant prices by estate agents, mainly to people from Cape Town who want a little place in the platteland.

Hennie Naudé used to run a coffee shop at Touws River. Whenever a train arrived, he would stand on the platform and call: 'Coffee! Coffee!'

At least there is still a visible reminder here of the old Trans-Karoo Express: opposite the station, next to the Flats of Venus, is the Trans-Karoo liquor store.

It's not hard to find old railway people in Touws River. In the Spar I ask a shopper whether he knows of any train drivers who still live in the town. He points to a man standing at the bread shelf, and says: 'There you have one.'

His name is Giepie van Zyl, and a few minutes later I find myself in his Nissan 1400 bakkie heading for the town's clinic where he's going to fetch another old railwayman, who's lost his legs to diabetes.

Along the way, Giepie talks incessantly. 'Do you know the Makkadas?' he asks.

The Makkadas was a famous train that used to run in this region between Laingsburg, Touws River and Ladismith. The writer Abraham de Vries, who grew up in Ladismith, has often written about the Makkadas in his stories.

During the Laingsburg flood of 1981, the Makkadas's railway line was washed away. It has never been rebuilt.

No one knows for sure where the name Makkadas comes from. Some say that a stoker once got bored with the slow pace of things, and encouraged the locomotive to 'Make a dash!'

Many trains had names in the old days: the Makkadas, the Tortoise Train (between Oudtshoorn and Klipplaat) and the Ghost Train (the night train between De Aar and Cape Town). Many people also referred to the daily train that ran between towns as the Milk Train, because it stopped at every siding to pick up cans of milk and cream.

'I was the last driver of the Makkadas,' says Giepie. 'We pulled out of Ladismith on the Saturday evening before the flood. It was already raining heavily at that stage. At some places we saw the railway line being washed away behind us.' Hy gesticulates wildly, and asks: 'Do you want to meet the conductor who was with me on that trip, then you can ask him yourself?'

We drive to another liquor store in the town. Oom Jan Stassen, the Makkadas's last conductor, is seated on a box outside the door. That was a terrible night, he says, when he and Giepie were travelling from Laingsburg ahead of the flood that was threatening to overtake them.

Then Giepie drives to the old railway offices. The buildings are empty. The windowpanes are broken, the roof sheets are missing.

'This was where we registered for each of our shifts.' He gestures in the direction of something that was once a well-polished wooden counter.

He looks at the decay around him. 'But you know what?' he says. 'I'm happy, I've had a good life. I've got good memories.'

It's late afternoon. I'm still here in Touws River.

At around seven o'clock, Giepie said, there's a train that can take me all the way to Cape Town.

I'm sitting on the platform. Life is change, and each generation has its own memories, I realise once again.

And on every train journey you discover new things.

'A rail journey is virtually the only occasion in travel on which complete strangers can bare their souls, because the rail passenger – the calmest of souls – has nothing to lose,' writes Paul Theroux. 'He has more choices than anyone else in motion.'

The sun is already low in the sky over the open veld. It's really quiet. Then there's some movement: a man comes walking from the direction of the empty station buildings, whistling a tune. 'Good afternoon,' I greet him.

'Good afternoon,' he replies and approaches me, still whistling. He's not so young any more and wears velskoene tied with thin wire instead of shoe laces. Johnny April.

We talk for a while. He also once worked on the railways, as a labourer. Then our conversation dries up. Johnny is standing before me, and I'm sitting, and together we're gazing into the vast expanse of the veld, saying goodbye to the day.

Later he produces a packet of BB tobacco and a folded newspaper page from his trouser pocket. He puts the packet of BB down on the patform and unfolds the page.

'Another suspect implicated in student's murder,' reads one of the headlines. But Johnny's not interested in that.

'How do you roll a zol?' I ask.

'You need a clean piece of paper if you want to roll a good zol,'

91

he says, and tears a white strip from the side. He crumples up the rest of the page and stuffs it into in his pocket.

Now he starts working on his zol. First he lays the strip of newspaper on the platform, then he takes the packet of BB, opens it, and sprinkles a neat little row of tobacco on the paper. In a measured way, taking his time, he starts rolling up the paper with his bony fingers.

'Your baccy shouldn't be packed too tightly,' he says. 'Your baccy must be nice and loose.'

He slides the rolled-up tube of paper in and out of his mouth a couple of times, lowers it again, and tests the condition of the tobacco by pressing the tube with his fingers. He does this delicately, almost lovingly. 'The bits of baccy must stick together in there,' he explains. 'If the bits don't stick together, you suck air.'

He puts the zol down gently on the platform, as if he's afraid it might break, and asks: 'Where're my matches?'

He removes a match from the box in his pocket, picks up the zol and jabs the match a few times into the one end.

'Your fire must be able to run through,' he says. He scrapes the head of the match along the side of the box, and then there's a flame, and then Johnny's cheeks become hollow as he sucks, and then there's smoke and the wild, tangy smell of zol in the air, and somewhere a korhaan is calling and the sun is painting the Karoo bushes red, the sky above us is the brightest blue, and a light breeze rises from the ground.

The whistle of a train rings out in the distance.

How glorious the earth can be at times.

The ship that refuses to die

The *Liemba* might arrive at ten o'clock, or at eleven. Or perhaps only this afternoon at four.

No one here at Mpulungu Harbour on Lake Tanganyika in the north of Zambia is sure – not even the harbour master, Whiteson Mubanga. 'One never knows,' he says; and then, almost by way of excuse, he adds: 'She's a very old ship, you know.'

Indeed. The *Liemba* is, as far as can be established, the world's oldest passenger ship still in use. She was built in 1912, and she sails from here to Kigoma in north-west Tanzania every week. It's a distance of more than 500 km, through the wild heart of Africa – Lake Tanganyika is bordered by Zambia, Tanzania, the Democratic Republic of the Congo and Burundi.

Theroux says that a voyage on the *Liemba* is a unique African experience. Photographer Ruvan Boshoff and I have come here to experience it for ourselves.

We've been waiting at Mpulungu Harbour since early morning with our heavy luggage. Our car, which brought us from Pretoria – three days, 2 983 km – will remain at the nearby Nkupi Lodge.

I have to say, it looks rather like we've come prepared for a long stay in a Gauteng state hospital. We have sleeping bags, plaster,

Dettol, energy bars, and a collection of pills that would make any hypochondriac envious.

The *Liemba* – pronounced Lie-hem-ba – departs from Mpulungu every Friday on a three-day voyage to Kigoma. That's what a woman working for the Zambian Tourism Board in Lusaka told us on the telephone.

There is no central booking office for the *Liemba*. We were able to establish the following on the Internet:

- Officially, the ship has room for six hundred passengers (but occasionally it carries up to one thousand).
- The *Liemba* has sunk twice.
- Congolese rebels have fired at the *Liemba* from the shore.
- The use of Valium or other tranquillisers is compulsory for passengers . . . Sorry, I'm only joking.
- The ship has first-, second- and third-class areas for passengers.

However, it's important to make that old Swahili motto your own if you want to travel on the *Liemba*: Hakuna matata. In other words, don't get yourself worked up about small things, such as punctuality.

Half past ten comes and goes, and then, some time after eleven, a small puff of smoke appears on the horizon. A while later, the tiny puff turns into a large, old ship with an asthmatic horn: Hooo-e-eee!

The *Liemba* is a total assault on your senses: all around us people shout and speak at once, the smell of fish and bananas hangs in the air, somewhere a goat bleats, and from a tiny transistor radio Lionel Ritchie's voice sighs: 'Dancing on the ceiling . . .' On the main deck, a few sad-looking chickens are tied to the railing with rope.

We've just clambered up from the pier by ladder with Paul Manaka, a Zambian harbour official. He helps us find a cabin, because here things are done differently to what happens in Durban Harbour. You don't buy a ticket – there's no ticket office. Nor is there a gangplank. In fact, there seems to be no order at all. Moments after the ship sounds its horn, hundreds of people suddenly descend upon the harbour as if from nowhere. Now everyone clambers over the railing onto the main deck by ladder, without any kind of control.

Paul Manaka knocks on a cabin door. A voice shouts something from inside.

'We wait a while,' says Paul.

It's exciting and somewhat strange to be in the middle of Africa, more than 1 000 km from the nearest ocean, on such a grand old ship. The *Liemba* is 70 m long and can officially carry 850 tons. On the main deck there are four first-class cabins, a dining room, a bar, a kitchen, bathrooms and toilets.

Below the deck, in the ship's bowels, are the engine room and the second- and third-class cabins. There is also a foredeck, and an upper main deck, where the bridge and the captain's cabin are.

We wait outside the closed cabin door. A succession of passengers squeezes past us. Some carry bags of dried fish on their head. We also see an old man with a goat on a rope, a man with a bicycle, and a woman holding a bunch of bananas. One guy even has a terrestrial globe in a plastic bag with him.

The *Liemba* isn't a cruise ship. For most passengers it's just transport. The shore of Lake Tanganyika is lined with tiny villages and hamlets, and the only way the residents can get themselves and their produce to larger places such as Mpulungu or Kigoma is on the *Liemba*.

Paul Manaka knocks again and opens the cabin door. Inside, in the dimly lit cabin, a man is sitting at a table with a book in front of him, which he appears to be reading: *Think Big* by Ben Carson. He introduces himself to us: 'Mister Mussa Baya, the ship's administration director.'

'No problem,' says Mr Baya. ' We can host you in two first-class cabins.'

It costs US$50 per person, first class, to Kigoma, no meals or drinks included. 'But you must first go for a security check,' says Mr Baya.

Huh? Security check? While everyone just boards and leaves the ship as they like? A short while ago I even saw a guy with a panga on board.

But we don't ask questions. We duly wait outside a tiny office Mr Baya points out to us. Inside, soldiers are searching and questioning four Americans who are hitch-hiking through Africa and are also on their way to Kigoma.

We're lucky. They interrogate the Americans for about 45 minutes; our 'security check' is much quicker, although a soldier methodically searches my bags, and even struggles through words like 'maltodextrine' and 'acesulfame' on the packet of Game in my backpack.

The first-class cabins are clean, and remind me of a train compartment. There's a sink and a tap with running (cold) water. The single bed has been freshly made with a sheet and also a pillow that feels like it's filled with a Western Cape telephone directory.

It is now shortly after three in the afternoon and we're still in the harbour.

I peer through one of the portholes. It's an exotic picture. Lake Tanganyika is the longest lake (743 km) in the world, and at 1 430 m, the second deepest (only Lake Baikal in Russia is deeper). Look north, and you see no land, only water. In the west, the mountains of the Congo form a dark line on the horizon, and somewhere on the foredeck that goat bleats again.

I leave the cabin and lock the door, because apparently the *Liemba* even has its own full-time thieves.

There aren't really tourists on the ship: only the four Americans (who immediately retreated to their cabin after the security check), a British woman and an Irish couple.

In the bar you can buy cold beer and cool drinks. Among the

drinks on offer are Castle, Kilimanjaro (a Tanzanian beer) and Zambezi (a Zambian beer).

'One thousand shillings,' says the man behind the counter. It's about R7. I give him 5 000 Tanzanian shillings, but he only gives me 3 000 change.

Meet Good Victor Mukuka, the *Liemba*'s barman.

Good Victor would probably have lost his front teeth to an angry fist had he been the barman in the Station Hotel in Boksburg, because Good Victor, you notice very soon after meeting him, almost always short-changes you. With a smile.

I sit down on the rear deck with a Kilimanjaro beer. Here I meet two other guys: the one seems to be a karate fundi, because he is energetically demonstrating a whole range of wild kicks and chops. 'Jean-Claude van Damme,' says the other one, pointing to his kicking friend. 'Very dangerous.'

Van Damme and Chuck Norris are great heroes in Africa, which is probably why so many African leaders behave like characters in a Van Damme or Norris movie.

I ask them about the ship's history, but they don't seem to know much about it. Jean-Claude just says gravely: 'This is a ship of history.'

He's right. The ship was built in Pappenburg in Germany, taken apart again, and in 1914 shipped to Dar es Salaam, Tanzania's capital, in about two thousand crates. It was the beginning of World War I, and Tanzania – or Tanganyika, as it was then known – was a German colony.

In Dar es Salaam the two thousand crates were loaded onto a train and transported 1 200 km to Kigoma at the lake. There the pieces were re-assembled, and in 1915 the ship was launched. But back then she wasn't called the *Liemba*. Her name was the *Graf von Götzen*, after a German governor of Tanganyika, and she was equipped with several cannons.

I look out over the quiet water. It's difficult to picture it, but during World War I there were naval battles between the Germans and the Allied forces on the lake, and this old ship took part in them. Because Lake Tanganyika has such a strategic location, each of the warring powers tried to control it.

But right now there's no time to think about the *Liemba's* past, because it sounds as if we're about to sail. Someone – hopefully the captain – has just pushed up the revolutions of the idling engine, and the wheezy horn coughs again.

There are probably five hundred people on board now, plus the goat, about forty chickens, and a flea market of baggage.

Then, slowly, the familiar world of the pier starts floating away from us and that goat starts bleating again.

We are now an hour from Mpulungu and sailing at a speed of about 9 knots – about 20 km/h – into the belly of Africa. Or that's what it feels like.

We stand on the foredeck at the ship's bow and across the lake the late-afternoon sun comes floating at us in thousands of pieces, while the *Liemba's* diesel engine chug-chug-chugs comfortingly below us, like a giant Lister engine, and a Muslim family on the upper deck kneels in prayer with their faces turned towards Mecca.

Somewhere behind us a rooster crows, the goat bleats, and a mother rocks a baby to sleep.

To the north of us, on the shore of the lake at the town of Ujiji in Tanzania, the historic meeting between the explorer David Livingstone and the journalist Henry Morton Stanley took place – the one where Stanley is believed to have said to Livingstone: 'Dr Livingstone, I presume.' (Some historians claim, though, that these weren't Stanley's exact words.)

Here on the *Liemba's* foredeck, with the warm wind fanning your body, you also feel a bit like a modern explorer, because this part of Africa is still so wild, empty and undeveloped.

A man comes up to us. His upper body is bulky and he wears glasses with large lenses that almost cover his cheeks. In his hand he holds a shiny ticket punch, like the ones conductors on trains carry with them.

Perhaps I'm just missing familiar old things, but all of a sudden he reminds me of Vause Raw, that plump South African politician of the long-gone New Republic Party.

'Vause' is the *Liemba*'s conductor. 'Nobody gets past me without paying,' he says.

Many passengers can't afford to buy tickets for a cabin. They pay about R30 to board, and then settle in somewhere on a deck or in a narrow passageway. There they sit, sleep, eat, and from there they get up to, well, use the first-class cabins' bathroom and toilets.

We ourselves haven't yet been in the bathroom and toilets. We've only walked past, too afraid to go in.

Michael Palin, the British TV travel programme presenter and former *Monty Python* star, took a trip on the *Liemba* a few years ago. The best cure for these toilets, he reckoned, was a hefty dose of Imodium, a drug that puts the brakes on the digestive system.

During our time on the ship, I discover that a five-step approach works best for dealing with the toilet issue:

1. Go to the bar and drink two beers for courage.
2. Get up and make sure you can squat on your haunches.
3. Fetch your own toilet paper in the cabin, stand in front of the bathroom door, and take a deep breath.
4. Barge in and, yes, that hole in the floor in the corner of the cubicle, that's where you're headed. Hold your breath, and admire the guys who've written the graffiti on the back of the cubicle door. They're really tough guys.
5. Do your thing, go outside, and start breathing again.

Palin isn't the only famous person who has travelled on the *Liemba*. In the 1930s the British writer Evelyn Waugh also sailed on it. The *Liemba* and her story was also the inspiration for CS Forester's novel *The African Queen*, about a ship by that name. The book was later turned into a classic movie, starring Humphrey Bogart and Katharine Hepburn – but it was in fact shot on another ship, on Lake Victoria.

Lawrence Green, the famous South African travel writer, sailed on the *Liemba* in the 1960s, and not much has changed since then. 'Her lower deck held at least 300 laughing, chattering Africans,' he wrote. 'It is a ship of bananas and dried fish, fowls and goats.'

Next to the dining room, outside the kitchen, one of the *Liemba*'s chefs, clad in a white jacket, has just untied one of the chickens, picked it up and taken it into the kitchen.

There's chicken on the menu tonight.

There's more than just chicken for supper, though. There's also fish, *nsima* (pap), tomatoes and bean salad – and the meal costs about R60.

But I'm thinking about that little chicken on the deck, and decide to skip supper and return to the cabin. I'm reading an interesting book: *Mimi & Toutou: The Bizarre Battle of Lake Tanganyika* by Giles Foden.

The book is about the history of the *Liemba* and the battle between the Germans and the Allied forces – especially the British – that raged here on the lake during World War I. The ghosts from the past are also on board the *Liemba*, and it's good to know about them.

Initially, the Germans controlled the lake. They patrolled the waters with this ship, as well as a smaller one, the *Baron von Wissman*. But in 1915 the Allied Forces decided to mount an assault on the lake.

Lieutenant-Commander Geoffrey Spicer-Simson of the British Navy and twenty-three men were sent to Africa. On board ship with them were two large motorboats, *Mimi* and *Toutou*, both specially equipped with cannons. At first Spicer-Simson wanted to call the two boats *Cat* and *Dog*, but his commanders wouldn't allow it. So he called them *Mimi* and *Toutou*, the French words for the sounds

100

a cat and a dog make. Spicer-Simson and his men landed in Cape Town, where *Mimi* and *Toutou* were loaded onto a train.

It took them about a month to get to Kisangani in the Congo by train. There the boats were offloaded, and towed overland in the direction of the lake.

I get up and go outside. A woman has unrolled her blankets on the deck in front of my door. She's fast asleep, next to a bunch of bananas. Everywhere dim light bulbs glimmer.

According to Foden's book, a young Afrikaans man helped Spicer-Simson and his comrades to load *Mimi* and *Toutou* onto two wagons, and hauled them to the lake with his oxen. Foden doesn't mention the young man's name. Who was he? Where did he come from?

While you stand here on the deck, you can't help but wonder: what were things like on this ship in 1915? Commander Gustav Zimmer, the captain of the ship at the time, would probably have been in his cabin at this hour.

Zimmer was the one who finally ordered the sinking of the *Liemba* – or the *Graf von Götzen*, as she was then known – on 26 July 1916. The Allied Forces were winning the war on the lake, and also in East Africa. The *Baron von Wissman* had been sunk by *Mimi* and *Toutou*, and this old ship had been hit and damaged by Belgian warplanes.

Zimmer didn't want the ship to fall into Allied hands, so he and his men sank her themselves near Ujiji, after covering all her important components in thick layers of grease.

For almost seven years she lay at the bottom of the lake, until 1923, when Winston Churchill ordered that she be brought back up. There seemed to be nothing wrong with her engines and other instruments.

About three months later, after everything had been cleaned and repaired, the ship began sailing on the lake once more – but now as the *Liemba*. This is what the lake was called in Livingstone's time.

Outside, people call out in Swahili. Loudly. Non-stop. Some of them whistle as well, and the goat is bleating again. Then the ship's horn goes, and we come to a stop.

I wake up with a start. It's shortly after midnight. What's going on? Could it be the Congolese rebels?

I get up and peek through one of the portholes. The ship's floodlights are on, and around us in the water a clump of small boats bob around, filled with people and all sorts of cargo. It's just one of the ship's regular ports of call.

The *Liemba* stops at fourteen places between Mpulungu and Kigoma. But there are no harbours. She stops about a kilometre or two from the shore, the anchor is dropped, and then the boats come closer, small ones and big ones, with or without engines.

Passengers climb down from the *Liemba* onto the boats, clutching suitcases and shopping bags and bicycles. Others climb up from the boats to the *Liemba*, with more bags of fish and cassava, a staple food here that resembles a sweet potato.

I step out onto the deck, wide awake. The famous Valiant rule clearly applies on the *Liemba*: there is always space for one more.

The man with the globe walks by. He's about to leave the *Liemba* for one of the smaller boats. In broken English he explains that he's a teacher in a village called Lagosa.

'Where did you get that?' I motion to the globe.

He takes it out of the bag and spins the earth around.

'She turns,' he says. 'You see?'

It's strange to be woken by crowing roosters on a ship.

It's a good idea to pack earplugs if you want to travel on the *Liemba*. Not only for the chickens. People start talking loudly in the passageway outside the cabin from early in the morning.

Several passengers arrived in the night. One of them, a woman, is very ill. She lies on a mattress opposite the dining room, emaciated, with large, despondent eyes. Her husband sits with her, in a T-shirt with 'Rough Rider' emblazoned on the front. He looks sad.

'It's her lungs,' he explains.

Something else happened in the night. That bleating goat on the foredeck suddenly went quiet. Did he go the same way as last night's chicken? We're too afraid to ask.

We go to the dining room. Breakfast is a rather tasty omelette, with something that looks like vetkoek, and a bowl of bean salad – all for about R40.

It's our second day on board, and below us the ship's diesel engine still chug-chugs away reassuringly.

After the ship was pulled back up from the lake bottom by the British in 1923, she was used as transport on the lake for a few years. But in the 1950s she sank again, in the harbour in Kigoma, because of rust and holes in the hull.

In 1970 the *Liemba* was lifted out of the water once more, this time with a crane. The hull was repaired and the old steam engine was replaced with a diesel engine. Ever since then, she has been doing duty on the lake just about full-time.

There are no deck games or other entertainment on board. You can watch recordings of Tanzanian soap operas on the two TV screens in the dining room. Good Victor (after probably handing you too little change for the Coke you've bought) is more than willing to translate from Swahili.

In Tanzanian soaps, it would seem, there are only two emotions at play – passionate love and uncontrollable anger. In a period of ten minutes the hero kisses the heroine four times, and slaps her twice.

I fetch my book and find a seat on the upper deck, on a bench in front of the captain's cabin. A short while later, a woman sits down next to me. Her lips are just a little too red and her top is cut a tiny bit too low, and she smells of perfume.

She winks at me and puts her hand on my shoulder.

Meet one of the *Liemba*'s travelling prostitutes. I quickly retreat to the lower deck.

The *Liemba*'s most famous prostitute was called Mila, Good Victor tells me later. She worked on the ship for more than twenty years. 'This ship is like a town,' he says. 'Everything you get in a town, you get here as well.'

There is no swimming pool on board, but no one stops you from diving into the lake when the ship stops. The water is clear and clean and the average temperature is 25°C (and if such things are important to you, the average pH is 8.4).

There are crocodiles and hippos in some parts of the lake, but generally they keep close to the shore. More than three hundred species of fish are found here.

Perhaps it's time to introduce ourselves to the captain. We knock on the door of the control room, but no one answers. We turn the door handle and enter. The bridge is clean and organised, and behind the steering wheel stands a man, his eyes fixed on an enormous compass.

To his left sits an older man on a high chair. He's playing the game 'Snake' on his cellphone. This is all you can do with a cellphone on the lake, because there's no signal. The man with the cellphone is Beatus T Mghaba, the *Liemba*'s captain.

Captain Mghaba has worked on the *Liemba* for twenty-eight years. He knows the ship's history well. 'Come and look here.' He walks to the compass. 'This is the original one.'

You can see the words clearly: Deutschland, 1912.

In the rainy season, from October to April, it can get quite stormy on the lake, Captain Mghaba tells us. Over the years, several smaller boats have sunk and their passengers drowned.

A few years ago, during a storm, the *Liemba* collided with another, smaller boat. Fortunately the crew were rescued from the water unscathed.

Now they have radar and a GPS device, he says, but ten, fifteen years ago they had to rely on their knowledge of the lake and this old German compass to navigate.

There were occasions when Congolese rebels fired at the ship.

This was in the 1990s, when they brought refugees from the Congo to Tanzania. Captain Mghaba stares ahead pensively. 'The *Liemba* is a lifesaver,' he says. It's estimated that the ship has brought more than seventy thousand refugees – yes, seventy thousand – from the Congo to refugee camps in Tanzania.

After more than a day on the *Liemba* you start realising Good Victor was right: the ship is a village on its own, with an onderdorp (third class), a bodorp (first class) and the rulers (the captain and Vause Raw with his ticket punch). And, as in all villages, you gradually become involved in everybody's business.

Some of the passengers are refugees from the Congo, Burundi and Rwanda. You hear of fathers, mothers and small children being hacked to death with pangas. You also discover a honeymoon couple from Kigoma on board, in second class.

Devlin Kamoto, a Congolese, tells me about Manba Muta, a giant crocodile that apparently lives in the lake. 'As big as a bus,' he says. How did Manba Muta get this big? He only eats the bodies of people killed in the wars of the Congo, Burundi and Rwanda, which are thrown into rivers and washed down into the lake.

The ill woman on the mattress outside the dining hall is not getting better. It doesn't look as if she's aware of anyone around her any more. Her name is Yemo Kasongo, we have since established. This morning the Irish couple prayed for her and made the sign of the cross in the air above her.

Earlier in the day someone accidentally trod on her hand.

And yet, the longer you are on this ship, the more you realise how much you still have to learn about Africa.

'To travel in Africa is to be confronted with the endlessly unfolding articulations of an elusive reality,' Breyten Breytenbach writes in one of his books. 'It is to travel in a mythical world of invisible powers, of dusty miracles, of taboos and drum language, and people who unroll the seamless fabric between the magical and a possible reality before you.'

It's late afternoon and we're back on the foredeck at the ship's bow, with the warm wind in our faces. The sun colours the water red, then almost blue, then silver.

I've stood in many places in Africa in the late afternoon: in the Knysna Forest and in the Namib, on those rocks above Port St Johns, at the Victoria Falls, in the Karoo, and on Clifton Beach, but nowhere have I ever felt as close to Africa as here on the bow of the *Liemba*.

Yet Africa is also a frightening place: in the Congo, on the lake-shore not very far from me, more than three million people have been killed in political conflict in the past eight years. Further north, in Burundi, the Hutus killed more than eight hundred thousand Tutsis in 1994. Many of the dead became food for Manba Muta.

Perhaps life in Africa is a bit like a Tanzanian soap opera: full of compassion and empathy one moment, and unbelievably cruel the next.

Is it possible to fall in love with a ship? Perhaps.

It's now about half past eleven on Sunday morning. It's our third day on the lake, and we're still about 100 km from Kigoma.

I even ate chicken last night (I think it had once been a reddish-coloured rooster).

At Muhale the ship drops anchor one last time, while the heavily laden boats float over from the shore and bob around us. Sometimes tourists get on or off the ship here. The Muhale National Park is close by, one of the few places in Africa where you can still see chimpanzees in their natural habitat.

There must be about a thousand people on board now. Everybody is friendly. It's just very noisy.

I stand on the upper deck and look out over the people. There are old ladies who have been sitting patiently with their bags of fish and cassava down below all the way from Mpulungu to sell their produce at the market in Kigoma, where they will earn about R70 for their efforts. There is a father on his way to his daughter's wedding. There are pickpockets and guys with karate dreams.

In Kigoma's harbour, after we moor, there's no immediate rush to get off the ship. Everyone first stands still and watches a few men lowering the desperately ill Yemo Kasongo, mattress and all, onto the quay.

We're going to spend two days in Kigoma, and on Wednesday we'll return to the *Liemba* and sail back to Mpulungu, where our car is waiting.

We walk to the lodge closest to the harbour, the Kigoma Rest House. Hot water and cold beer, at last.

The woman at reception insists that we fill in the register separately. You are asked to write down your name and address as well as the tribe you belong to.

I think of the nights in the humid breeze on the bow of the *Liemba,* I recall the story of that nameless young Afrikaans man who helped Spicer-Simson get his boats to the lake. And I think of those nine generations of Snymans here in Africa, and that distant uncle of mine who'd moved to Kenya as far back as 1905.

Then I lift the pen, and in the space below 'tribe' I write: 'Afrikaner'.

Oom Jan Mobil's hoekie

Something's wrong: *7de Laan* ended more than fifteen minutes ago, and Jan Mobil still hasn't arrived at the bar of the Lutzville Hotel in Lutzville on the West Coast.

'It's strange,' says Boetie Fox, the barman. 'It's bloody strange.'

'Oom Jan's probably first gone to the café to buy cigarettes,' the guy on the stool next to me reassures him.

Boetie looks at his watch. 'Maybe.'

The guy next to me is called Fanie or Danie. Or that's what it sounded like when he introduced himself to me a moment ago. I couldn't hear very well, because Boetie had Kurt Darren singing a bit too loudly through the loudspeakers: *'Sê net ja-a-a . . .'*

Only three of us are currently here in the bar: me and Boetie and Fanie-or-Danie.

We're waiting for oom Jan Mobil, a retired oil salesman from the town.

'Oom Jan will be here just now,' says Boetie, looking at me. 'I think I must close the windows in the meantime. Oom Jan doesn't like a draught on him.'

Boetie emerges from behind the counter with Iesh, his English bulldog, at his heels. In the corner, slightly to the side above an empty stool, a sign reads: *JAN MOBIL SE HOEKIE*.

Oom Jan has sat here in his own special corner for the past thirty-four years, every day, six days a week, week after week, year after year, drink after drink, in times of joy and in times of sorrow.

Yes, Jan Mobil deserves an entry in *Guinness World Records*: the man who has sat on the same stool in the same bar every day for more than three decades. The regular to beat all regulars.

Just after half-past nine in the morning oom Jan reports here at the hotel. First he drinks a cup of black coffee with two spoons of sugar at reception, where Netha, wife of the owner Frans Fox, is on duty. At ten o'clock, when Boetie opens the bar, he moves across there and stays till about lunch time. Then he goes home to rest.

At night, just after *7de Laan*, oom Jan is back at his post in the bar.

Boetie closes the windows behind us one after the other. For more than four years he's been barman at this hotel which belongs to his father, a retired policeman – and as behoves any good barman, Boetie's developed a sixth sense for anticipating people's needs.

'Are you still okay?' He points to the glass in front of me once he's back behind the counter. 'Another one?'

I decided more or less on the spur of the moment to travel to Lutzville after someone in Paternoster, about 200 km south of here, had told me about oom Jan. I'd like to meet oom Jan, I decided, because, well, why would anyone want to visit the Lutzville Hotel every day for thirty-four years?

The bar looks no different from hundreds of others around the country: the bottles hanging upside down against the rack, together with all the usual paraphernalia: the caps, the ties, the Blue Bulls flag, the photo of Joel Stransky's 1995 drop goal, and the statuette of Johnny Walker with his sword in its sheath.

We hear the sudden noise of a car outside.

'That's oom Jan,' says Boetie, as he bends over the fridge and takes out a bottle of naartjie-flavoured Energade. This is the only drink oom Jan indulges in nowadays.

A few moments later, the door swings open and shortish oom walks in with a packet of Lexington in his hand. His feet know the route well, past the dartboard, past the notice on the wall that reads: *Moet asb. nie stompies op die vloer gooi nie, dit brand die klante se hande en knieë wanneer hulle huis toe gaan* (Please don't throw cigarette stubs on the floor, they burn customers' hands and knees when they go home).

'Hello, oom Jan,' says Fanie-or-Danie next to me.

But oom Jan doesn't return the greeting. Not yet.

Oom Jan walked in here for the first time in 1973. This was just after he'd resigned from the police in what was then South West Africa, and moved to Lutzville.

The people of this region are partial to nicknames, and it wasn't long before he became Jan Mobil. Because he worked for Mobil.

Boetie places the Energade in front of oom Jan, who still doesn't greet us. First he takes all the odds and ends from his trouser pocket and arranges them on the counter in front of him together with the Lexington packet: a lighter, a purse, a bunch of keys – as if he's getting ready to address a meeting.

Then he looks in our direction, and says: 'Good evening, manne.'

Boetie and Fanie-or-Danie return his greeting: 'Good evening, oom Jan.'

If there'd been a 'happy hour' in the Lutzville Hotel tonight, it would probably only have lasted ten minutes; the rest of the time it would have been unhappy hour. Or that's what it feels like. No one talks much. And damned Kurt Darren isn't even singing any more.

A guy in a John Deere T-shirt has just walked in and ordered a whiskey and water. Now he leans over to Fanie-or-Danie, and asks: 'What did the dyslexic Satanist write on the wall? Hey?'

'I don't know,' replies Fanie-or-Danie. 'What?'

'I love Santa.'

110

No one laughs, including the John Deere guy. Oom Jan tilts his head back and sucks on the bottle of Energade. He used to be a whiskey drinker. 'But three years ago the doctor ordered him to lay off the booze,' Boetie had informed me a little earlier.

Nowadays, oom Jan sticks to Energade. Sometimes, just sometimes, he gets reckless and challenges his constitution with a glass of undiluted Coke. But still, oom Jan is here every day, in his corner, with a new, healthy Star King apple glow on his cheeks.

'Anyone who thinks a bar is just a drinking place has never been lonely.' What wise man said that? Ernest Hemingway? Koos Kombuis?

I get up to introduce myself to oom Jan. He points to the empty stool beside him. 'Sit.' I sit down. It seems as if oom Jan is about to make a weighty pronouncement: he taps his fingers on the counter, clears his throat – but says nothing.

Regulars like oom Jan often don't talk very much.

'There must have been many different barmen since the time Oom first started drinking here?' I try to make conversation after a while.

'Yes,' replies oom Jan. 'Ye-e-e-s. Many. Many.' Then another silence descends, during which time oom Jan keeps glancing at the door next to the counter, as if he's waiting for a platoon of words to burst in and come to his rescue.

'In the beginning there was a barman called Van Zyl,' he says after some time. 'After him came old Coenie Truter who always ordered coffee for himself, and then added three tots of brandy.' He pulls a Lexington out of the packet, but doesn't light it. 'Who was it again that came after old Coenie? Ag man, I can't remember.'

At first oom Jan just dropped in at the bar in the evenings after work, but since retiring about eleven years ago, he's started clocking in in the mornings. He's only absent on Sundays, and when he goes to Henties Bay on his annual fishing trip. (He's made this trip twenty-eight times.)

Years ago, in a somewhat surprising turn of events, he was ab-

111

sent from the bar for two days after a certain Richard Nel had beaten him up.

It seems as if oom Jan is trying to suck words from the Lexington.

'We used to call him Grumpy, that Richard.' He waves at the cloud of smoke that surrounds him. 'That guy was really grumpy. One night I was just sitting here, then he came and stood next to me. "Yes, old Jan," he said. "Yes, old Richard," I replied. The next moment he punched me. With his fist. Flat on the floor.

'Then I just got back onto my stool. But before long, there was Grumpy again. "Yes, old Jan," he said. Then he bashed me again.'

Oom Jan lets the Lexington rest in the ashtray in front of him. 'That night he nearly beat me into a pulp, old Grumpy.'

Apparently Grumpy took a dim view of the fact that oom Jan used to be a policeman, but oom Jan didn't hit back. He's not the belligerent, loud-mouthed type. Jan Mobil is the quiet man in the corner, the one sitting in his own cloud of smoke gazing into space over his, well, bottle of Energade. He's, well . . .

'It's not always nice at home on one's own,' he says. 'It's not nice.'

It's getting late. Outside, swarms of beetles circle around the street lights, and a dog barks somewhere.

The guy in the John Deere shirt has gone home, and Fanie-or-Danie has just got to his feet: 'I have to skedaddle, boys. My wife's waiting for me.'

Oom Jan remains seated. He was once married, years ago, but while he served as policeman on the Angolan border in the old days, certain things happened that he'd rather forget. He's now divorced.

'I've probably spent three-quarters of my life sitting in this place,' he says suddenly. 'But you know what?' His eyes are bright blue. 'I'm happy here.'

Here, where Boetie sees to it that no draught reaches his shoulder blades, which are sensitive to cold.

Here, where he's always surrounded by voices.

112

Nine hundred Harleys at Colesberg

At Smit seems a little disillusioned. 'There's a guy here who's brought his poodle along,' he says, and feels around for the bottle of Old Brown Sherry next to him. He takes a swig and lowers the bottle again. 'Can you believe it? A *poodle*. At a *bike rally*!'

It's hard to believe, yes, because a bike rally isn't supposed to be the kind of outing where you bring your Maltese along, is it? As we know, these are affairs where guys drink too much, do doughnuts with the back wheel of their bikes on the tarmac in front of the local hotel, and ogle late-night wet T-shirt competitions in the beer tent.

But that's not how things work here at the annual Harley-Davidson Rally at Colesberg in the Karoo. This is a classy event.

At, who has his own transport company in Bellville, may be standing here behind the library in Colesberg's town centre swigging OBS straight from the bottle, but he's the exception. To all appearances, he's one of the wilder offshoots here. Most of the others with him are drinking whiskey from silver goblets. Or, hang on - Harley riders don't drink whiskey.

Harley riders drink Jack Daniel's.

And Harley riders don't light their cigarettes with a lighter. They use a Zippo.

Colesberg is ready for the Harleys. Some streets here in the town centre, where the offices of the New National Party quite appropriately share a building with an undertaker, have been closed specially for the occasion. The *Colesberg Advertiser en Karoonuus*, the local newspaper, carries a report about the rally – on the same page as two stories about the centenary celebrations of the ACVV, the Afrikaanse Christelike Vrouevereniging.

A stage has been erected here, as well as a bar, a workshop and a temporary Harley boutique where you can buy anything from a pair of Harley braces (R400) to that must-have Harley leather jacket (R3 000 plus).

Because that's how it works. Even though you already have a Harley, it can easily set you back another R7 000 to look like a real Harley rider: leather boots, leather trousers, belt, shirt, jacket, dark glasses, and that bowler hat crash helmet that reminds one a bit of the potty under great-grandma's bed.

Harley people are special. Diagonal Insurance Solutions now have a special Harley insurance policy.

Old At takes another swig from his OBS bottle and looks in the direction of a bloke in a Hell's Angels jacket who's just got off his Harley in front of the Wild Steer restaurant with the requisite air of stony-faced determination. One wonders what these hard-core bikers would say about the alleged presence of a poodle here at the rally.

By yesterday the first Harley riders had already started roaring into Colesberg from all directions across the Karoo, more than nine hundred of them, from Polokwane in the north to Upington in the west. Johannesburg. Durban. Port Elizabeth.

There are also two guys from Soweto here, and an Iraqi with the surname Hussein who throws his hands into the air and shouts 'No! No! No!' when you ask him if he's related to Saddam Hussein. 'I'm *Hayder* Hussein. Not Saddam!'

But not all of them have ridden their Harleys to Colesberg. Some have transported their Harleys on a trailer behind their BMW X5s, their new Ford 250 bakkies or their Jeeps. Others, like André and Ursula Venter from Pretoria, towed their Harleys to Bloemfontein and then rode the 220 km or so to Colesberg.

This is the fourth time the rally is being held here, and for Harley riders it is more or less what the Argus Cycle Tour is for cyclists.

It's now about eleven o'clock on Friday morning – the rally is held over three days, Thursday, Friday and Saturday – and on the face of it not much is happening yet: At is drinking his OBS, the others their Jack Daniel's. The bloke in the Hell's Angels jacket is now sitting on a chair next to his Harley opposite the Wild Steer restaurant, surveying the world around him with a long, implacable Hell's Angel stare.

Well, perhaps I should go and find out what he thinks about the poodle.

I walk up to him. He is heavily tattooed. I greet him. My own reflection in his dark glasses returns the greeting. No, he doesn't want to talk. Not about the poodle, and not about anything else, for that matter. 'No comment, sorry,' he says. 'We don't talk to the media.'

Then he shifts his fierce gaze to where a man holding a small camera is approaching. Every now and then the man stops next to a parked Harley and photographs it.

The photographer is Frits Cloete, who works in the butchery at the local Score supermarket. 'Aren't they too beautiful for words, Meneer,' he says. 'I've already snapped twenty two of them. But I hear there's a gold one here! Has Meneer perhaps seen it? *That* one I want to snap.'

The biggest part of a Harley rally consists of standing or sitting around and looking at your own and other people's Harleys. Or this is what it looks like at the moment.

Everywhere in the main street, especially in front of the Bordeaux coffee shop near the Dutch Reformed church, Harley riders are looking at Harleys. 'That's because no two Harleys are the same,' says Paul Moore, a businessman from Johannesburg.

You get different Harley models: Fatboys, Softails, Road Kings and Sportys. But for some or other reason, most Harley riders aren't satisfied with the ordinary model. They want theirs to be different.

They have a word for it: customise. This means that you buy a Harley for R180 000 plus, and once you own the bike, you start buying other parts and accessories at the Harley shop, or order them from overseas on the Internet: handlebars, seats, footrests. Until you think the bike is as beautiful and unique as it can possibly be.

Paul has already customised his Fatboy to such a degree that the screws are just about the only original parts left of the bike he'd bought. Here in the town hall a Harley show is on the go where you can vote for the customised Harley you consider to be the most beautiful. The bikes are also judged on aspects such as neatness, accessories and workmanship.

The bike entered by Richard Proudfoot of Pretoria looks a bit like Mr America, the Harley in the cult movie *Easy Rider*, which starred Dennis Hopper and Peter Fonda.

'Customising a Harley is an art form,' says Proudfoot, whose Harley is worth more than R450 000. 'I begin with a frame, then you fit other panheads and slash cuts and build him up into something you can be proud of.'

Harley people have their own lingo: panheads (engine type), slash cuts (exhaust pipes), Lynchburg lemonade (Jack Daniel's), and so on.

But there's one thing about a Harley that can't be customised. It's that distinctive sound the engine makes when it idles: potato-potato-potato. Or is it perhaps: putu pap-putu pap-putu pap?

A few years ago, Harley-Davidson's head office in America even tried to patent that distinctive sound, for fear that manufacturers in the East would start producing fake Harleys that sound just like the real McCoy.

That putu pap-putu pap sound is caused by the unique, rather old-fashioned design of the engines – a design that has changed little since William Harley and Walter Davidson built the first engine in Milwaukee, America in 1901.

Harley engines have only two pistons, explains Richard Proudfoot, and those two pistons are on either side of a single crankshaft. As soon as the engine is switched on, those pistons start galloping up and down: putu pap-putu pap . . .

They may just stand around, inspecting each others' Harleys, but does this mean Harley people are a tamer species than bikers who participate in the Buffalo and Rhino Rallies?

Harley people are wild. But in the style of the *Ruiter in Swart*. The horseman in black, Ben Brand – hero of those photo books we furtively read in the seventies – would arrive at a bar on his horse Midnight, slowly dismount, purposefully push open the doors, saunter in – and order a glass of *milk*.

Many Harley riders stop here in front of the Bordeaux coffee shop, observe the scene from behind their Harley dark glasses, get off their bikes purposefully, enter heavily gloved – and order coffee. With hot milk, please.

Okay, that's a generalisation. Not all Harley riders are designer-crazy. Nor are most of them obsessed with status and keen to show off. Among the bikers assembled here are doctors, lawyers, business people, accountants, poodle lovers (I still haven't managed to track him down). But you have to look fairly decent when you ride a Harley. The bike deserves it.

'You can't ride a Harley in tackies,' says Pieter Groenewald of the Steelwings Club in Pretoria. 'Harley-Davidson is a way of life. Our club meets three times a week. We're one big family.'

Most Harley riders don't take themselves too seriously, either. 'I've always wanted to be wild,' says André Venter from Pretoria, and smiles. 'With my Harley I can now at least pretend to be wild. Maybe I should get myself a few stick-on tattoos.'

Oom Kallie du Preez, once chief game warden of the Etosha game park in the old South West, is here as well, together with his wife. They've ridden all the way from Parys in the Free State.

'I don't have much time for guys who transport their Harleys to the rally on trailers,' he says. 'I believe you get three types of Harley riders: those who've loved Harleys since childhood, those who dream of Harleys, and those who like to show off.'

Oom Kallie owns fourteen Harleys and sometimes gets calls from people overseas who're experiencing problems with their bikes' engines. 'I know a Harley's engine better than old Chris Barnard knew the human heart,' he reckons.

It's now Friday night, just past eleven o'clock, and at a Buffalo Rally the strip show would have been in full swing with guys demanding full nudity, and starting to chant: '*Wys, wys! Wys jou muis*!'

Here at Colesberg, a fellow has at least done a quarter doughnut with his Harley in front of the open-air stage where the Jesse Jordan Band is performing. (For bikers, a doughnut is roughly the equivalent of a century in cricket or a hat-trick in rugby or soccer.)

On top of that, another bloke has ridden through the front door of the Wild Steer on his Harley Heritage Softail. 'Jan,' he introduces himself. 'Jan Diener. Just call me Lekker-ou-Jan.'

Lekker-ou-Jan hails from Cape Town, and earlier pitched his little tent next to the stream in the centre of town. He's clutching a bottle of Delgado liqueur. 'Here, take a swig,' he orders, and checks me out as if he wants to customise my face. 'It's mother's milk.'

'Do you always drink Delgado?' I ask.

'No,' he replies. 'Just at rallies.'

Lekker-ou-Jan would have considered doing a full doughnut 'if the bloody tyres weren't so expensive'.

The Hell's Angel who this morning refused to comment on the rumoured presence of a Maltese poodle at the rally is now standing at the counter in the Wild Steer. He has mellowed somewhat. His name is John, he says, but he doesn't want to reveal his surname.

Obtaining reliable information about the Hell's Angels is no easy matter. If you look on the Internet, what you discover about the South African Angels more or less amounts to the following: one of the founder members was called Moose, and at one time Japanese bikes weren't allowed in the club.

The Hell's Angels are synonymous with Harleys, but in the seventies the Harley-Davidson company in the United States took a deliberate decision to distance itself from the Angels' rough image. But this almost meant the end of the company. In the early eighties the company was on the verge of bankruptcy; no one wanted to identify with a bike ridden by tame, little grey men.

In his book *Outlaw Machine* Brock Yates describes how Harley-Davidson then decided to start marketing the image of the wild Harley rider – designer wild. It paid off. Today the company's turnover is in excess of R13 billion.

Yates also recounts how hard it is globally to obtain reliable information about the Hell's Angels. He's right. Even here in Colesberg, John remains tight-lipped.

But in the meantime, Lekker-ou-Jan Diener has progressed to the counter of the Wild Steer with the front wheel of his Softail. Now he spins that Harley, vrrooooooooom, until the glasses on the table vibrate and clouds of smoke hang in the air.

Calm returns. 'It smells just like fish,' says Susanne Meyer, a manager of the local Wimpy Bar, who is also sitting at the counter.

It's early morning in the Merino Inn, a motel just outside town, and a moment ago I was woken by the barking of a small dog. Now I'm just lying here in room D9, thinking of everything that happened the night before. The quarter doughnut. The uncommunicative Hell's Angel. (Though he did eventually allow me to inspect the flame-like tattoos on his arms.) The golden Harley that I can't track down. For a while I also searched unsuccessfully for Uli Schmidt, one-time Springbok hooker, after someone had sworn that he'd spotted him, bandana and all.

Lekker-ou-Jan's spinning with his Softail had gone off quite smoothly, but later in the evening he found that someone had stolen his tent next to the stream.

Then the dog barks again. I can hear it's in the room next door, and it sounds as if a male voice is saying: 'No, Wollie!'

A while later I discover that At has been right about the poodle: the man in the room next to mine is Tommy Moolman, a Harley rider from Cape Town, and he and his wife brought their Maltese to the rally in their bakkie. And her name is not Wollie, but Miss Molly.

Yates Brock may be mistaken. In *Outlaw Machine* he contends that what Harley-Davidson sells, is the chance for a 40-year-old accountant to don black leather, ride through small towns and scare people.

But the Karoo people aren't scared of the Harley people. They feast their eyes on them.

It's now Saturday morning just after nine, and about two hundred and thirty Harley riders are on their way, via Middelburg, to Teebus, site of the entrance of the tunnel connecting the Fish River with the Gariep Dam. I follow them in my car.

They want to ride their Harleys in that tunnel.

I have to confess: when you see the Harleys riding like that on the open road, you wish you could afford one yourself. That low seat, that putu pap-putu pap sound, the wind in your face, and the *Easy Rider* thoughts all this evokes. Damn, it must make you feel a bit like the hero in your own movie.

'Many guys will tell you that a Harley isn't really even a good motorbike,' says Burt Moss from Durban. 'Maybe they're right, though I've had no problems with my Softail. A Harley is also not an exceptionally fast bike, but there's just something about a Harley that's different. My Harley is my freedom.'

At the turn-off to Middelburg at least five local residents with video cameras stand waiting for the parade, and when the bikes stop in the town, it seems as if the whole dorp has turned up to watch.

Pat, a local hairdresser who also inserts belly button rings (she tells me that she's done more than a hundred rings in Middelburg), stands on the pavement in front of her salon together with her husband Sebastiaan. 'Have a look at that, Lollie,' she says to him. 'Just look at them getting eye drops.'

A special ambulance has accompanied the procession, and some Harley riders are getting a dose of eye drops from the paramedics because their eyes have dried out from the cold wind blowing in this area. (Pat claims that the wind is connected with Hurricane Rita that is raging in America.)

Pieter Kahts, the only Harley owner in Middelburg, and his wife Hendrina join the others on their ride to Teebus, because it's not every day you get the opportunity to ride in a tunnel like that.

From the entrance, the tunnel slopes down as it runs under a mountain. Slowly, they ride down it for about 800 m, turn around, and then race back quickly, bursting into the light to the applause of a crowd of local people.

It's rather a pity that old Whitey Brits and the other miners from Welkom who so eagerly attend the Buffalo and Rhino Rallies on their Kawasakis, Yamahas and Hondas couldn't be here today, as I've long held the theory that miners enjoy bike racing so much because, for large parts of their lives, they work in narrow tunnels under the earth. This ride would have been very liberating for old Whitey and the others, as it would probably have felt a bit like racing out of West Driefontein's No 7 shaft.

Every bike rally has its own climax.

At the Rhino Rally it's usually the Saturday afternoon, when the brandy kicks in and the guys start spinning doughnuts and doing wheelies and burnouts, and the Odendaalsrus miner's chick gets on the back of his Kawa Ninja stark naked.

At a Rhino Rally in Orkney I once heard a guy at a tickey-box arguing with his wife, and at one point shouting at her: 'Okay, okay, just don't have kittens or an otter, you hear me?'

It's now half past three on Saturday afternoon here at Colesberg, and everything is proceeding sedately and stylishly. No sign of anyone having a kitten, let alone an otter.

In front of the Bordeaux coffee shop, everyone is standing around once again, drinking Jack Daniel's or coffee, and inspecting each others' Harleys. Hayder Hussein has just had to deny again that he is related to Saddam – he's in South Africa in search of a better life and works at the Harley Centre in Cape Town. Tommy Moolman is also here, but he has left Miss Molly at the motel.

The more you socialise with Harley people, the more you realise that they're actually just ordinary, extremely civilised people who like doing what they enjoy – and who dream a little, as any other motorcyclist does, of taking to the road in pursuit of freedom, like Dennis Hopper and Peter Fonda in *Easy Rider*.

At the Dutch Reformed church some distance away, people in their Sunday best are entering the building because there's a wedding on in town this afternoon.

And then, a while later, the unexpected happens: a biker comes roaring along from the direction of the town hall and, as true as Bob, when he's more or less opposite the Bordeaux, the guy raises the front wheel of his bike off the ground and wheelies almost up to the church.

It's Dave Eager from Johannesburg. But he's not riding a Harley. It's a Buell – though the Harley-Davidson company does have a stake in Buell. You could say Buell is Harley's youth league, because Dave now performs all the customary Buffalo stunts while the Harley people applaud him. He wheelies, then comes to a stop with an elegant doughnut. One of Colesberg's street children runs up to the bike and touches its hot back tyre. A policewoman takes a photograph with her cellphone.

Then the biker roars off again and disappears round the corner.

On the stoep of the Bordeaux everyone almost immediately becomes quiet and sedate again, as if he'd never been here.

As befits a Harley rally.

The Richtersvelders' great trek

Tant Kowa Uys sighs heavily and points with her kierie to the area outside her front door where a few goats are grazing among the stones. 'Ja, child,' she says. 'This old Richtersveld is a harsh world, there's no doubt about it. Here you learn to trust your God.' She lowers the kierie. 'But, trek? – no, I won't trek again. This is where they'll bury me.'

For more than forty years she's lived here in Eksteenfontein, about 90 km north of Port Nolloth, in a small whitewashed house much like those of some of our great-grandmothers: an old black Dover coal stove in the kitchen, portraits in wide oval frames on the walls of the dining room, a pitcher on a washstand in the bedroom.

Tant Kowa is eighty-seven and still bakes her own bread, wears a real old Voortrekker bonnet on occasion, and sometimes sings long-drawn-out Dutch hymns after family prayers. 'I've travelled a long road, child,' she says. 'I can tell you many stories.'

I'm here to listen to those stories because I'm exploring the Richtersveld, that empty strip on the map between Steinkopf and Port Nolloth up to the Orange River. South Africa's only real desert, some call it. It's a world of quiver trees and rare succulents, jackals and puff adders, a raging sun, diamonds and copper, and solitude. Especially solitude. That's why it's particularly the people of this region that interest me. How did they end up here? Was it of their own free will? And how do they survive here between the stones and nowhere?

Apart from the bigger towns – Steinkopf, Port Nolloth and Alexander Bay – there are only three other tiny dorps in the area: Eksteenfontein, Lekkersing and Kubus. But most travellers who visit the region come to the Richtersveld National Park and drive past these dorpies, or they don't stop for long. It's easy to become so absorbed by these open spaces that you forget completely about the nearly five thousand people who live here.

Eksteenfontein, where I'm chatting to tant Kowa, is the most remote of these dorpies. It has a post office, two or three shops, a lovely church with a bell tower, and a library where Etienne Leroux's highbrow novel *Een vir Azazel* cuts a solitary figure among the Ena Murray love stories.

The people who live here call themselves the Bosluis Basters. They are the proud, pious descendants of Khoi people and whites who'd trekked from the Cape – and they speak a uniquely beautiful Afrikaans. To capture its texture, their language almost needs to be rendered phonetically.

'Let me tell you where Eksteenfontein got its name, child,' says tant Kowa and rests her hands on her knees. 'Our history comes from *nientienhonderd* (nineteen hundred), you know. Our forefathers were all mixed up with the whites. Went to the same church as them, everything. My late ma was baptised in the Dutch Reformed church in Vanrhynsdorp, *verstaat* (you understand)?

'Then, in *nientienhonderd* and three, the Church said to us: Look, you are a different sort of people, baster people, we can't have you with us any more. You'll have to find another place for yourselves. Then, all at once, we had no school and no church.'

Tant Kowa's people had no choice but to load their possessions onto their donkey carts and start trekking. North. Into the wilderness.

124

Hannes Meyer, the owner of the farm Bosluis in the district of Pofadder, had allowed them to outspan on his land. But there wasn't room enough for all of them, and their donkeys and livestock.

Dominee Eksteen, their minister, had made representations to the government, but it was only in 1948, after twenty-one years of trying, that the government informed them, yes, there was land for them. At Stinkfontein in the Richtersveld.

Tant Kowa's people and about forty other families inspanned their donkeys again, this time for their last trek here, to their Canaan.

It wasn't an easy decision for everyone. Floors Strauss, also resident in Eksteenfontein, had told me earlier about the hard choice that confronted Hannes Meyer. 'My Oupa Meyer had to choose: if he wanted to keep his farm, Bosluis, in Bushmanland, he had to be a white,' he told me. 'If he wanted to come to Eksteenfontein, he had to give up his status as a white and become a coloured. In the end he became a coloured.'

Tant Kowa's grandmother, Johanna, nearly a hundred years old at the time, was part of the trek. 'We had to load old people like her onto the wagons,' recounts tant Kowa. 'Our animals we herded along.

'Every morning along the trek the women had to get up, put a bit of meat on the fire if there happened to be some meat. Or they smeared a piece of bread for the *kinnertjies* and then gave them a *koffietjie*.' While the little children had their bread and their few drops of coffee, the goat was milked right there, next to the fire.

'And then the men had to get up and go looking for the donkeys and inspan them,' tant Kowa continues, 'and I caught the chickens and put them in the cage that hung underneath the wagon. This was our way of life.'

After twenty-eight days on the trail, they stopped here among the barren hills of the Richtersveld. 'Over there we put up our tent houses,' says tant Kowa, and again points out the door with her kierie. 'There was nothing here, just a bit of water that stood there, a small fountain.'

Stinkfontein.

One of the first things they did was to change the name of Stinkfontein to Eksteenfontein, in honour of Dominee Eksteen who'd helped to negotiate this barren piece of land for them.

Tant Kowa falls silent for a while, then sighs. 'And that's how Eksteenfontein got its name.'

Yet not all the inhabitants of the Richtersveld are Bosluis Basters. Nama people also live here, and the San and the Khoi have lived here from time immemorial, especially further north towards Kubus, near the Orange River. And of course the region also attracted missionaries. Dr Walter Richter of the Rhenish Missionary Society, after whom the Richtersveld is named, had already arrived in the 1830s. Over time, the Bosluis people, the Nama, as well as others with a thirst for adventure, have become so intermixed that nowadays it's hard to distinguish one group from the other.

Tant Kowa's father, who was white, spent the last years of his life here at Eksteenfontein. Uys, Cloete, Meyer, Farmer, Strauss, Joseph – these are common surnames in this area.

Deon Joseph, a local livestock farmer, lives near tant Kowa. He's among the privileged of Eksteenfontein: he owns a car, one that resembles a cross between a railway trolley and a beach buggy. 'What you see here is a pipe car,' he says proudly and points to the apparition. 'I bought it from a guy in Steinkopf. For R3 000. He built it himself.'

We approach the car for a closer inspection. Yes, it's a fitting name: a pipe car. Because the body consists of what looks like a collection of pipes, with an asthmatic Toyota 1300 engine, without a bonnet.

'The other day I accidentally drove over the air filter, that why it's rattling so much,' says Deon. 'But I put in a new tydpot.'

'Tydpot?' I ask. 'What on earth is that?'

Deon taps the distributor. 'Here it is.'

Afrikaans people, these, indeed.

The Richtersveld may be sparsely populated, but there are few other places in the country where you find so many hitch-hikers. I'm now on my way from Eksteenfontein to Kubus, and I've hardly left the town when he materialises in the stony wilderness: the ubiquitous Richtersveld Hitch-hiker.

I stop. His name is Hannes Cloete, another livestock farmer. He's on his way to his brother's funeral in Kubus and is carrying a fake Adidas bag from which peeps the neck of a quart beer bottle. (Earlier this morning outside Port Nolloth I'd picked up a guy who was on his way to the same funeral, but at the turn-off to Lekkersing he wanted to get out as he had a few matters to attend to there first.)

It's understandable that there should be so many hitch-hikers. The region covers more than 5 000 km² and most people don't have cars, not even a pipe car. And if you drive in this part of the world it's important to have enough petrol, as well as an extra spare tyre. There are no filling stations, nor is there cellphone reception. How did Floors Strauss describe it again this morning? 'Here you can hear the silence. Here you can distinguish between something and nothing.'

The road is in poor condition, but it winds through spectacular stony koppies and mountains, while Hannes, who is uncommonly talkative for a guy on his way to his brother's funeral, acts as guide: 'That one is Tatasberg. And to the other side is Bobbejaanswanhoop. They say that's where a baboon once grabbed one of her kinnertjies by the tail as it was about to fall over a precipice.'

From a distance this region looks wild and empty, but it has all kinds of trails and caves and old prospecting sites. You especially discover this when you read Karl Reck's *Tracks and Trails of the Richtersveld*. This book and Fred Cornell's *The Glamour of Prospecting* are probably the best sources for finding out more about the history of the Richtersveld.

Years ago the late Gert Nieuwoudt, a legend in these parts, had a small shop here between Kubus and Eksteenfontein, which are about 100 km apart. People say that Gert discovered an enormous chunk of copper in the mountains near De Hoop. He broke this block up into smaller pieces by using a blowtorch and explosives, then packed the copper pieces into drums and rolled them down the mountain, where they were loaded onto a wagon.

Whether this is true or not is hard to say. Tales about legendary copper deposits and mythical diamonds are rife. Somewhere in the vicinity there's also supposed to be a place called Bushman's Paradise. Fred Cornell, who did prospecting work here in the early 1900s, looked high and low for Bushman's Paradise, a fascinating search that he describes in his book.

The story goes that a soldier had deserted from the German forces fighting in the old German South West Africa. Then he lost his way. He was on the brink of dying from thirst and hunger when he came across a group of Bushman people. They gave him food and water, and once he'd regained his strength he made tracks again.

But the German soldier again lost his way, and died of thirst.

His corpse was found by a German patrol. They also found the diary the soldier had kept as he travelled – and a leather pouch bulging with diamonds of various sizes.

In his diary, the soldier wrote of the fabulous treasures he'd seen among the Bushman people who assisted him. The Bushman children, so he said, played marbles with the diamonds. But heaven only knows what became of that German's diary.

'I don't know Boesman Pêridaais,' says Hannes. 'Is it near Kubus?'

Among South African towns, Kubus is probably the one with the greatest variation of spellings of its name: Kubus, Khubus, Khuboes, Kuboos, Xuboos, Xoeboes, Koeboes.

And it seems that no one in the town is sure what it means.

'My grandmother said it means the fountain of the lord in Nama,' says a fellow in front of the closed door of the tourism office. 'Maybe the old woman was right.' Others reckon that the name is derived from the Nama word for brackish water.

Kubus – this is the most common spelling – is not much bigger than Eksteenfontein, and from far off you can see its beautiful white church. Most of the adults who live here do one of three things: they are livestock farmers, they work on one of the diamond mines in the region, or they are unemployed. Especially unemployed.

And, as tends to happen in many other places as well, the unemployed while away much of their time in bars and pubs. Not that you can just do as you like in a Richtersveld pub: many of these establishments have warnings of all kinds stuck on their walls. In Steinkopf's pub, for instance, there are ten handwritten rules – or rather commandments – that you have to obey if you want to quench your thirst without being disturbed:

1. No persons under the age of 18 years allowed.
2. No loafing around allowed on the premises.
3. No liquor from outside allowed on the premises.
4. No weapons allowed on the premises, trespassers shall be prosecuted.
5. Misconduct shall not be tolerated, trespassers are subject to expulsion.
6. Every person shall subject him-/herself to searching at the gate.
7. No sitting around inside pub. Seating only for people who buy.
8. No dancing allowed in the pub.
9. No bare feet or slipslops allowed.
10. No smoking inside pub on carpet.

A few years ago, the communities of Kubus, Eksteenfontein and Lekkersing instituted a land claim on a large part of the land from here to Alexander Bay, about 40 km from Kubus. Initially the Land Claims Court dismissed the claim, but about two years ago the Constitutional Court in Johannesburg ruled that the state and the mining group Alexkor had to officially return an area of 85 000 ha, including the mineral rights, to the communities.

The court found that the Richtersveld people and their ancestors had, over the years, been driven away from the land to make room for diamond mines. It also found that the Richtersvelders were entitled to compensation for all the years that diamonds had been removed from their land. Huge amounts are being mentioned. Millions.

'Someone even said we can get billions, but that's not true,' says Floors Strauss of the Richtersveld community association that had lodged the claim. 'We want to be very realistic. It won't help if we suddenly turn a few people into millionaires and in ten, fifteen years' time the community is still struggling. We rather want to invest money in projects that uplift the community in the long term.'

Of course the Richtersvelders are glad about this. But the many years of hardship have made some people cynical. They say they'll wait and see what happens.

Floors and others are still negotiating with Alexkor. The company may possibly continue with its activities, but the Richtersvelders will share in the profits. In future they want to concentrate on tourism in particular, says Floors. One of the places that can be developed better as a tourist attraction is the Richtersveld's so-called Wondergat, a mysterious sinkhole.

The Wondergat is about 15 km outside Kubus, on the road to the Richtersveld National Park. (Keep your eyes peeled, the turn-off sign on the left is small and faded.) In the distance lies Cornellsberg, the highest peak in the Richtersveld (1 377 m), which was named after Cornell.

It's a strange place, this Wondergat. The opening measures approximately 10 m x 5 m. No one around here can explain its origins. It also seems that no one knows exactly how deep it is.

'They say that a cold breeze blows from the hole,' says Bennie Matthys, yet another hitch-hiker I picked up a while ago outside Kubus. He's travelling to a cattle post near Sendelingsdrif, where his family lives.

I hold my arm over the hole. No cold breeze.

Some Nama people believe that the hole is the home of a big snake. With a diamond in its forehead.

Years ago, Gert Nieuwoudt and the late oom Kosie Farmer from Eksteenfontein used a rope to help one Flippie van der Westhuizen to descend more than 30 m into the hole.

Flippie went down the hole on two other occasions as well, and each time he became seriously ill afterwards, writes Japie Coetzee in his book *Bakens na Brandberg*. 'Was this due to the unhealthy, stuffy air?' asks Coetzee. 'Or was it the revenge of an angry ancestral Nama spirit?'

Eastwards from Kubus, towards the interior, the landscape becomes increasingly empty and more mountainous. Bennie, who is in the car with me, was born at a cattle post in these parts and he knows every koppie and drift by name. Rosyntjieberg, the Vyf Susters, Skilpadsand.

Every livestock farmer has his own post, and allows his sheep and cattle to graze in accordance with old, unwritten rules. Near Sendelingsdrif Bennie indicates that I must slow down. There on the open plain lies their cattle post: a small round house, a cooking shelter, a kraal made from branches.

He's welcomed almost like the Prodigal Son. Two little ones come running up to him. 'Did Oom bring us some sweets?' they shout.

An old woman emerges from the small house and mentions coffee, and Bon Jovi sings in a crackling voice from the transistor radio hanging from a branch in the cooking shelter.

The northern part of the Richtersveld was declared a national park in 1991. The park is unique for two reasons: it's a diamond mine, and in terms of an agreement between the livestock farmers and the park authorities, seven thousand sheep and goats are allowed to graze here. Nowadays it also forms part of the Ai-Ais-Richtersveld Transfrontier National Park.

The gate is at Sendelingsdrif, about 40 km from Kubus. There's a good campsite and air-conditioned huts at Sendelingsdrif, but I decide to push on to De Hoop, where there's also a campsite.

The condition of the road worsens. You should preferably not visit this area in your family car. The road snakes between the mountains before you slowly start crawling up Halfmensepas.

As the name of the pass suggests, this is also the region of the rare halfmens (*Pachypidium namaquanum*), a strange succulent with a half-human shape whose 'head' always faces north. A Nama legend provides an explanation for this phenomenon. In earlier times, when their ancestors were chased southwards over the Orange River by Khoi tribes, the Namas say, some of the people looked back and immediately turned into trees – just like Lot's wife in the Bible was tranformed into a pillar of salt.

But botanists have a different explanation: because in winter the days are shorter and the sun follows a low arc across the horizon, the top parts of the plants turn towards the north to take in as much sunlight as possible.

The campsite at De Hoop on the banks of the Orange River is beautiful. It's late afternoon, the water silently flows past, and there's a wistfulness about the halfmense with their northward gaze.

People once lived here at De Hoop: Oom Paul Avenant, his wife Daisy, and their children. Two of the little ones, Susanna and Gloudinatjie, died here of illness. Here they farmed with livestock, planted sweet potatoes, and held church services under the trees.

Oom Paul reportedly had a Chev bakkie known as the 'Sardine Tin'. But in 1960 the Avenants, as well as the Graaffs, Rupings and a few other white farmers of the district, had to move off their farms. The government had decided to turn the area into a so-called coloured reserve.

From De Hoop you can also drive back to Sendelingsdrif via a longer circular route, over the Tatasberg range, through Kokerboomskloof, down the Helskloofpas – 4x4 territory. (Oom Paul Avenant helped build this pass with his Sardine Tin.) But you won't meet a soul along this route. Therefore I decide to drive along the river to Alexander Bay, past Brandkaros and Bloeddrif.

The Rupings – who, like the Avenants, were forced to move away – lived at Beesbank, near the place where Hendrik Louw had in 1925 shot the last hippopotamus in the Orange River. (No memorial has been erected for the hippo.)

Near the Rupings's family cemetery, there's a homestead next to the road. I turn in there. A man peers through the screen door. Oom Jan Mostert. His wife, tant Elize, has probably the biggest collection of fridge magnets in the Richtersveld.

Oom Jan, who has also built himself a pipe car, farms for a mining company here next to the Orange; because, yes, some of those farms people were evicted from now belong to the mines.

'Many people come knocking on my door,' says oom Jan. 'A lot of them are Gautengers who've had accidents with their cars on this road. They always speed, don't they?'

Sometimes he also gets visitors who sit and chat for a long time about this, that and the other, only to ask eventually: 'Oom, does Oom perhaps have any diamonds we can buy?'

The closer you get to Alexander Bay, the more diamond stories you hear: how diamonds are hidden in pieces of wet biltong, in the hubcaps of cars, in the hollowed-out soles of shoes . . .

You can't just drive into Alexander Bay. The town is surrounded by a high fence, and you have to fill in a form at the access gate. There are shops and a guesthouse and a video store. In the pub at the angling club, a throng of men stands around the counter. A guy introduces himself as Spook Goosen; he's lived here for years.

According to Spook, it's not always easy being an angler here. 'When we come in from the sea,' he says, 'the mine's security people X-ray our fish to see whether we haven't hidden any diamonds inside them.'

Spook rests his elbows on the counter. 'Do you know how you spot a diamond detective?' he asks.

'No,' I say. 'How?'

'They always have braai grids and Coleman cool boxes on the back of their bakkies,' he says.

I'm now on my way from Port Nolloth back to Eksteenfontein, and from there to Vioolsdrif, after I'd had far too good a time last night in the company of Spook Goosen.

The hitch-hiker who stands waiting outside Port Nolloth is called Frans Cloete.

The singer and songwriter David Kramer tells how he once picked up a hitch-hiker here in the Richtersveld who was carrying a fold-up Christmas tree. This was the inspiration for his song 'Die pad na Lekkersing'.

'How did Lekkersing get its name?' I ask Frans.

'This was a very festive area,' he says, and gazes over the plain.

But this is not why the town was called Lekkersing. Apparently the old residents gave it this name because the sound of the flowing water in a fountain at the town was so beautiful to them.

Just as she was three days ago, tant Kowa is still sitting on her sofa at Eksteenfontein. I think again of what she said: 'Don't look down on someone who has fallen. Maybe God spared you the fall because he knew you wouldn't be able to get up again.'

The dorp reminds me in a way of the country towns I grew up in: here there are also broken-down cars in the yards. Here, too, there are ooms who try to keep a vegetable garden going, despite the lack of water and the voracious koringkrieks. Here there are also houses with Sunbeam-red stoeps and lopsided garden gates and mongrels lying curled up at the front door.

And of course, the name of the town appears in stones packed on the side of the mountain.

I stop at the house of oom Jan and tant Miemie Strauss, two of the town's oldest residents. Oom Jan comes walking across the yard with puffs of dust rising behind his velskoene. Tant Miemie is busy in the kitchen, and against the wall of the lounge hangs a motto that once hung in so many Afrikaans homes: *Ek en my huis, ons sal die Here dien.* (My family and I, we shall serve the Lord.)

Oom Jan points to a chair and says I should sit and make my-self at home. But it's not really necessary for him to say this: I already feel at home in this house that looks so much like my great-grandmother's. I also understand exactly what oom Jan means when he later says: 'I've tried in the past to leave this place, but after a few days I long for the mountains and the dryness and the stones.'

The Forest still guards its secrets

No one seems to know where the Knysna Forest's elephants are.

At Fisanthoek, Josie Hancox directs me towards Diepwalle, and at Diepwalle Wilfred Oraai points in the direction of Kom-se-bos and Gouna. At Karatara, again, oom Ernst Zeelie, a retired forester, just shakes his head and says he's never seen an elephant in all his years in the Forest. But Leon Kitching, who lives a few streets from oom Ernst, has tangible proof that the Forest's three elephants exist. Or are there four of them? Or perhaps only two?

'Eileen!' he shouts down the passage of his house. 'Ei-leeeeeen!'

'Ye-e-s, Pa,' replies a child's voice.

'Just bring Pappie that plastic bag on the cupboard!'

A few moments later a young girl enters the kitchen with a plastic bag in her hand. The neighbours' two little girls are peeping over the lower half of the door. Tant Issie van Rooyen, Leon's mother-in-law, takes a long pull on her cigarette.

Leon takes the bag from the child. He pushes his hand into it and produces a dried ball of dung.

'Oom Ool,' he says.

A friend of Leon's had found it the other day near Goudveld in

136

the Forest and brought it to him. Many people have come to look at the dung, because the Forest's elephants stir everyone's imagination – the Forest people as well as the people of the outside world. The 'oolfante' – as some of the old people in these parts still call them – are among the Forest's many secrets.

Knysna's Forest is written with a capital F. Dalene Matthee, author of the famous Forest novels – *Circles in a Forest*, *Fiela's Child*, *The Mulberry Forest* and *Dreamforest* – first began capitalising the word, and when you start walking and driving around this landscape, you realise that this is how it should be.

The Forest, says oom Ernst, is bigger than the people.

The Forest is not just one place. It stretches more or less from Mossel Bay, past George, Wilderness and Knysna, past Storms River and Plettenberg Bay almost as far as Humansdorp. It all forms part of the famous Garden Route; although for most people the Garden Route is just the N2 that runs along that part of the coast.

Few people travel from Avontuur over the Prince Alfred pass through the Forest to Knysna. And few take the Seven Passes road from George into the Forest. Fewer still take the turn-off at Wilderness onto the dirt road past the lakes to Karatara, a forestry station and village about 55 km from Knysna.

Not many outsiders really know the Forest people. Some even look down on them.

'They call us patatboer,' says tant Issie, rubbing the circles round her eyes. Next to her, Leon Kitching shakes his head. He doesn't understand it. They look after their children. Their house is clean.

A plate with a motto hangs on the stoep: God bless this house. Tant Issie has read the Bible thirteen times from beginning to end. 'The Bible doesn't jump around,' she says. 'It starts at one point and carries on right through to the end.'

To experience the Forest properly, two things are indispensable: a good map of the area and some knowledge of the Forest people's history.

In the 1860s, where George is situated today, there was already a forestry station manned by nineteen forest workers who cut wood in the forests. Yellowwood. Stinkwood. Blackwood.

It is estimated that there were about four hundred elephants in the Forest in 1876. At first the wood was used to make wagons, later to build ships, especially for the British navy, and subsequently also for railway sleepers. Then the furniture factories appeared on the scene – and after this nothing was quite the same in these parts.

According to oom Ernst Zeelie, one of the people who provided Dalene Matthee with information for her Forest books, it's important to distinguish between the old forest workers, or woodcutters, and the foresters. 'The forest workers were people who survived by living in the Forest, cutting wood and selling it to timber merchants,' he says. 'The foresters were people like me. We worked for the department of forestry and earned a salary.'

But the woodcutters and the foresters did have one thing in common: hardship. Even though the foresters received a salary, it was a mere pittance. Unlike the foresters of today, they were in fact just manual labourers who often had to cycle long distances to work.

Several retired foresters live here at Karatara: Oom Ernst and oom Oubaas Terblans and oom Sakkie Oerlemans. You'll often see them sitting on the stoep in the late afternoon, faces turned towards the Forest that blankets the spine of the Outeniqua Mountains. Many of them carry the scars of falling logs and stubborn branches. Several hands lack fingers which were once claimed by an axe or a saw.

They all have stories to tell. Stories of hardship, in particular. Of the many nights they slept in the Forest under shelters built from branches during chopping time. How they often had to survive for days on just coffee, home-made bread and perhaps a few sweet potatoes. How scared they were of 'oolfante'.

Oom Oubaas – like many of the others – wasn't even eighteen when he first entered the Forest with an axe in his hand. They had to fell the specially marked trees and saw them up into logs. Then, with the help of donkeys and mules, they had to drag the enormous logs to where the trucks – and before that, the ox wagons – could collect them.

'At first your hands ached really badly, ou broer,' says oom Oubaas, who is sitting with his wife Hester on the stoep of their small house. 'In the mornings before starting work again, you dripped hot candle wax onto your hands. This and paraffin helped to harden your hands.'

Many of the forest workers were exploited by the merchants, as Matthee clearly shows in her books. Early in the twentieth century the government began to 'close' more and more parts of the Forest because many of the forest workers cut wood indiscriminately in their attempts to make a living.

Most of the old forest workers have died off by now. Like the elephants. That's why a trip through the Forest has a nostalgic feel. Near Rondevlei there's a grave near the road: 'Christiaan Roelofse. Born 8 October 1875. Died 14 February 1951. Rest in peace beloved father of children.'

Everywhere, you stumble upon the graves of the old Forest people. The same surnames recur: Zeelie, Botha, Stander, Terblans. Often the headstones are overgrown, as if the Forest is trying to reclaim them.

'I live near the Forest,' writes Dalene Matthee. 'You drive for kilometres through farms, pine plantations and scrub, and you ask yourself: what happened to the primeval forest that once stood here?'

Today we have strict conservation laws, but over the decades large parts of the Forest have succumbed to development. Trees were chopped down left and right and sold to merchants. The elephants were also widely hunted for their tusks.

'I'm one of the last of a generation,' says oom Chrisjan Botha, a cabinetmaker, in his workshop at Rondevlei. 'I'm one of the few people born here who are still alive.'

He shakes his head. 'Nowadays this area is infested with Germans.'

It's not that oom Chrisjan has anything against Germans. He just means to say that a lot of German citizens have bought property in the area around Rondevlei and Hoekwil near Wilderness. Strictly speaking, this isn't part of the actual Forest, but oom Chrisjan and many of the old folk who lived here could still be called Forest people.

Like many of the old folk, he calls George 'Ge-org' as if it were an Afrikaans name. 'I do get to Ge-org now and again,' he says, 'but I've never visited Johannesburg, Durban and those kinds of places.'

In fact, at the moment he's making another lounge suite from stinkwood – which these days costs up to R15 000 per cubic metre – for someone from Durban.

Oom Chrisjan, who has also sacrificed a finger to his craft, gets up from his chair. He wants to show me something. We drive up the steep slope at Rondevlei, heading back towards Karatara.

A signpost to our left: Von Kaske. German. Situated in an open space, with the most beautiful view over the lakes and the far-off sea, is a small, old Dutch Reformed church, a replica of the Geloftekerk, the Church of the Vow in Pietermaritzburg. The inscription on the cornerstone reads: *`Tot eer van die Here en ter herinnering van die Gelofte van die Voortrekkers op 9 Desember 1838 by Danskraal en herhaal op 16 Desember.'* (In honour of God and in remembrance of the Vow the Voortrekkers made at Danskraal on 9 December 1838 and repeated on 16 December.)

'This is where I was baptised, confirmed and married,' says oom Chrisjan, 'but now the Church has gone and sold the place.'

It's now a Lutheran church, for the local German community, with some of the old Forest people's graves at the back – overgrown by long grass.

'There you have it,' says oom Chrisjan. 'There you have it.'

It's a near-perfect title for a book about these parts: *Circles in a Forest*. Because it's not really possible to travel in straight lines here.

You're on the way to Goudveld when you hear about the cabinet-maker at Rondevlei, so of course you turn back. And now I'm driving to Karatara for the second time, because here at the lakes Silas Brand has just told me about a man with twelve fingers in Karatara.

Leon Kitching should know him. And indeed he does. The twelve-fingered man is Herman Julien, the handyman at the local school.

But twelve fingers aren't all that strange, says Leon. 'My ma also had twelve, but the doctor amputated her extra ones. She kept them in a bottle of formalin for donkey's years. She was a Beukes, and it runs in their family. He pauses for a while. 'We're six brothers and one sister, and half of us have twelve fingers.'

Perhaps the gift of twelve fingers was the Forest's way of compensating the woodcutters for the loss of so many fingers to axes and saws.

In the olden days, some Forest people had all kinds of superstitious beliefs. Such as the notion that a blue duiker's gallbladder is situated in its head – Dalene Matthee writes about this in *Circles*. Others believed that snakes, particularly puff adders, get their poison from toads.

And when a child was born with a caul – the so-called *helm* – it was a very serious matter, writes Greta Gericke in a dissertation about the religious development of the region's Afrikaans-speakers. 'The caul is removed and dried. Then it is ground finely and given to the baby to ingest. So that later, when the baby grows up, he or she would not see visions.' Or so it was believed.

But oom Ernst Zeelie tells me they no longer believe these kinds of things. They are Christian people. As an elder, he himself has twice had the privilege of attending sessions of the synod of the Dutch Reformed Church in Cape Town.

Herman Julien is not at the school. He's on his way home on his bicycle.

Herman is a friendly fellow with an angelic facial expression. He gives me a gentle twelve-fingered handshake. 'The Lord made me like this,' he says with a rather thick tongue. 'And I love the Lord.'

It's hard not to think of Matthee's characters when you travel your own circles through the Forest.

At last I've left Karatara and am heading in the direction of Diepwalle, Gouna and Stanley-se-draai, the birthplace of Saul Barnard, the main character in *Circles*. The Forest around Knysna is known as the Great Forest. But first I want to stop at Millwood.

This was where they dug for gold once upon a time. Some of the diggers' houses and other buildings have been restored and may be visited. It's also worth the trouble to call at Portland Manor, the estate of Henry Barrington, who's one of the pioneers of this region and a character in Matthee's *Mulberry Forest*.

If you ask any of the old folk in these parts, they'll tell you that until relatively recently, Knysna used to be a sleepy little town. Nowadays, the line of cars queuing to get into town stretches kilometres. Fairly ordinary houses fetch prices in excess of a million rand.

On Thesen Island, where there used to be a sawmill, there is now a big property development, and at the old quay where the forest workers sold their wood you can eat oysters in any one of numerous restaurants. The part of the Forest where oom Ernst Zeelie and his cronies used to hunt bushbuck has become a golf estate.

Outside Knysna, on the way to Diepwalle, a road sign warns: 'Wild elephants roam in this area. Enter at your own risk.' But before I can get to Diepwalle, a forestry station in the heart of the Great Forest, my route takes me in yet another circle. To Fisanthoek, to visit the Hancox family who I've heard about from someone at Keurhoek. They're said to be staunch Forest people.

And, yes, Josie Hancox is surely the closest thing to a real-life Saul Barnard one could hope to meet. His mother, tant Eveline, lives in a tiny old wooden house, and his late grandma, a cousin of his late grandpa, lies buried in the front garden, barely ten paces from the front door.

Josie and his brother, Tommy, speculate in wood. Like Saul Barnard, Josie apparently has trouble finding happiness in love. He recently had a potential bride flown in from Russia.

He sits down on a log in front of the house and starts telling the story of himself and this Russian girl – and this could easily be part of another Forest novel. After she had stayed here in Fisanthoek for a while, the girl went back to Russia. Josie's world and hers were just too different.

The whole episode, he says, set him back R40 000.

At first they thought there was only one elephant left in the Forest. Then two more were spotted. But now they're perhaps down to two again. No one knows for sure.

Or, at any rate, Wilfred Oraai, a game warden at Diepwalle, doesn't know for sure. But if he doesn't know, it's likely that no one else would; for the past sixteen years it's been his job to try and trace the elephants in the Forest, follow them and photograph them.

'About five years ago we still thought there was only one old bull left,' says Wilfred, who's just emerged from the Forest with a small backpack over his shoulders. 'We hardly ever saw him.

'Then, in 1994, the park's people decided to bring in three young cows for the bull from the Kruger National Park. This plan didn't work well. One of the cows soon died of pneumonia. It was probably too wet and damp for her here.

'The remaining two managed to meet up with the other elephant.' Wilfred smiles wryly. 'But then we discovered that that elephant wasn't a bull at all. It was also a cow.'

The two remaining Kruger elephants were caught a few years ago and resettled in the Shamwari game park in the Eastern Cape. Because they couldn't adapt to the damp Forest, they had started invading the nearby agricultural areas and caused much damage.

But then one day Wilfred and his colleagues discovered that the cow they'd mistaken for a bull wasn't the only original Forest elephant. There were two more, a bull and a cow. 'We first found their tracks near the Knysna River, and then we started following those tracks.'

Wilfred walks between 25 and 30 km a day through the Forest. But it's still a struggle to track them down. It's now April, and he last saw the elephants on 12 December. Or at least the younger bull and cow.

'It's been quite a few years since we last saw the old cow,' he says. 'We think she's still alive, but we're not sure.' He laughs again. 'Of course, its always possible that there may be other elephants in the Forest besides these three.'

In the Forest anything is possible. Visitors often believe there are fairies living here, Wilfred tells me. At Sedgefield there's also a bunch of present-day hippies who sometimes see their own version of fairies.

In the Forest there's room for everyone.

'You should tread softly when you work in the Forest,' Dalene Matthee says somewhere, 'and if you've paid close attention, you'll be filled with respect when you leave.'

With oom Fanie Pad through the Moordenaars Karoo

Oom Fanie Stadler has just polished off two slices of toast and a mug of alarmingly strong coffee. Now he's ready to go and show me the Moordenaars Karoo. 'Come,' he says. 'Let's go.'

He walks out of the back door of his administration house here in Laingsburg. 'Do you have enough water?' he asks, and blinks his eyes against the glare.

Yes, I have enough water. I've also brought along dried fruit and two tins of tuna, just in case. But most important: I have *him*, oom Fanie – Fanie Pad – at my side, and he's going to show me the Moordenaars Karoo.

The Moordenaars Karoo is a bit like, well, the famous G-spot: everyone knows about it, but no one's really sure where exactly it is. I started my search for it by asking people in Prieska, more than 500 km north of here. They directed me towards Kenhardt. But in Kenhardt, someone said I should rather ask around in Carnarvon. While there, I watched the horror movie *Nightmare on Elm Street* in the company of the barmaid of the Carnarvon Hotel, just to hear later, no, sorry, the Moordenaars Karoo is still further south.

After short visits to Loxton and Beaufort West, I stopped here in Laingsburg. I went to the municipal offices to ask where the Moordenaars Karoo is – and chanced upon oom Fanie Pad chatting to Abrie du Toit, the local health inspector, in his office.

Oom Fanie, whose nickname means Fanie Road, was a grader driver, road maker and foreman for the Cape roads department in this region for donkey's years. He knows the roads of the Moordenaars Karoo like the back of his hand, and he's offered to go and show me what's what. But he just wanted to grab a bite to eat first. He's also changed his clothes for our trip. Velskoene, short pants, and, in case we get lost, people would be able to spot us from far because he's now wearing the brightest of canary-yellow shirts, with a black badge on the front: Laingsburg Pigeon Club.

'Come on. Let's get going.'

09:30: Heading for the veld

There are no towns or Ultra City garages with restaurants in the Moordenaars Karoo (or 'Moornaarskaroo', as they call it in these parts). That's why it's a good idea to have something to eat before you head out.

It's probably also advisable to pay a visit to Abrie, the health inspector, before you set out. He'll show you on the surveyor's map against his wall precisely where the Moordenaars Karoo is situated, because the region isn't identified on ordinary road maps.

Or you could always ask oom Fanie Pad to be your guide. Oom Fanie, who retired five years ago, doesn't only know the area; he's also full of wise advice. He's just informed me that Black Label beer is an excellent cure for feet that swell as a result of too much fluid in the body.

'Turn right here,' he indicates just after we've crossed the bridge over the Buffels River that flows through the town. There's the sign: *Moordenaarskaroo R202*. At least I now know that it lies north of Laingsburg.

There are various theories about the origin of the name, 'Murderer's Karoo'. Some people maintain that, many years ago, a bunch of convicts escaped from a prison – apparently in Worcester – and chose the area as their hiding place because it is so remote. (Sloet Steenkamp, a character in the popular Afrikaans TV series *Arende*, lay low in the Moordenaars Karoo after the Anglo-Boer War because he refused to swear allegiance to the Crown.)

But others claim that this scorchingly hot and arid part of the world was named 'Murderer's Karoo' for the murderous nature of the climate.

After a short distance, the tarred surface of the R202 changes into a bumpy dirt road. 'Just look at all the stones in the road,' oom Fanie complains. 'In my day it didn't look like this. The new people don't know how to grade properly.'

The road winds like a snake trail through dusty hills and then, about 10 km outside the town, there's another bridge over the Buffels River. This is the Excelsior Bridge, and oom Fanie Pad helped to build it.

'I tell you, here I sweated like hell,' he relates. The river bed is dry, but if you dig a shallow hole in the soft sand the water will start seeping into it, he says.

The name of the Buffels River is mentioned with awe in these parts. This is the river that in January 1981 swept away most of Laingsburg when it was in spate after a cloudburst. The Moordenaars Karoo seemed to live up to its deadly name that day, as most of the water that roared towards Laingsburg came down from this area. Oom Fanie's father was among the one hundred and two victims that drowned in the flood.

The world lies wide and empty around us. The veld is covered with bushes that oom Fanie points out as if they were old friends of his. Kraalbossie. 'Sheep get dropsy when they eat it.' Vyebos. 'If you braai wors over it, the bush makes it taste very good. It puts that Karoo taste into your mouth.' Granaatbos. 'If you boil it in water and give that to your pigeons, they fly like hell.'

About 15 km north of Laingsburg we reach a T-junction. If you go right, you go to Beck-se-vlak. 'Turn left here,' motions oom Fanie.

I turn left and stop the car. Somewhere a bustard calls asthmatically. 'If the korhaans call,' warns oom Fanie, 'the wind's going to blow.'

There are piles of stones everywhere, as if they've been packed here by someone. Some people say you get ash-coloured ghosts here that move across the earth like whirlwinds. And these aren't just ordinary ghosts – you come across them in the daytime, too.

'We're now at the mouth of the Moordenaars Karoo,' says oom Fanie, and points towards the open spaces ahead. 'Here old Jan Arendse once overturned one of our trucks – it was a wreck.'

10:15: Into the heartland

The further you drive from Laingsburg, the more it feels as if the Moordenaars Karoo could be a kind of Bermuda Triangle where all sorts of strange, inexplicable things happen, or once happened in the past.

Some people believe that this is indeed the case.

Dr Cyril Hromnik, a historian of Slovakian descent who lives in Cape Town, believes the Moordenaars Karoo was once inhabited by the so-called Quena people. The Quena were apparently descendants of an Indian people who worked in ancient mines in southern Africa before the 1500s, in present-day Zimbabwe and at Barberton in the old Transvaal, among other places. Later, they supposedly moved to the Karoo. According to Dr Hromnik, many of the stone walls one sees in the Moordenaars Karoo are the remnants of Quena temples.

The piles of stones, Dr Hromnik claims, are primitive observatories which the Quena people used with the help of the stars to determine direction. Dr Hromnik brings tour groups to the area from time to time, and points out all kinds of places to them.

No, says oom Fanie, he doesn't know anything about the Quenas.

11:00: Not a town in sight

We are now about 25 km north of Laingsburg on the R202, the dilapidated main road of the Moordenaars Karoo. There are no signposts, but this is no problem because oom Fanie Pad knows the name of every spot we pass: Knoffelfontein, Skelmhoogte, Dikboompies.

Oom Fanie also provides a running commentary on all kinds of topics. 'You don't grade a road, you "cut" it. Grading is something a farmer does with a tractor,' he says. And: 'There are guys at Laingsburg who give their pigeons drugs to make them fly better.'

Beyond Ouberg we descend into something that looks like a much smaller version of Namibia's Fish River Canyon. The Buffels River winds through slowly, unhurriedly, eroding the soil as it has for centuries. From this vantage point you can see a large part of the Moordenaars Karoo, which in fact is a rather small region.

Take a map and draw an imaginary triangle in the open space between Laingsburg, Merweville and Sutherland. This, more or less, is the Moordenaars Karoo. But take note: Merweville and Sutherland *don't* lie in the Moordenaars Karoo, as any of their inhabitants will tell you. These towns are situated in the Koup and the Roggeveld, respectively.

And neither do Laingsburgers really consider themselves part of the Moordenaars Karoo. The Moordenaars Karoo is solitary, apart, and probably the only region in the country without a principal town. About twenty years ago, there were still thirty, forty farmers who farmed in the Moordenaars Karoo. 'Today there are only seven or eight left,' says oom Fanie.

11:15: Lynxes and ticks

In the road ahead of us walks a man, with puffs of dust rising around his ankles. He carries a roll of blankets on his back and a bag in his hand. 'Stop the car,' says oom Fanie. 'Have a chat with him.'

It's good advice, because a region such as the Moordenaars Karoo exists largely in the words of its inhabitants. As a traveller, you may be overawed by this still, barren world, which nevertheless reveals nothing of the region's history. There are neither museums nor monuments here. There are some graves here, but graves all tend to speak the same sombre language, regardless of their location.

In his book, *Karoo,* the well-known travel writer Lawrence Green, who drove through here in an old crock of a car in the 1950s, writes that the first settlers trekked from the Cape to these parts in the eighteenth century. 'They were the restless spirits, the toughest of the tough . . . They lived with their families in tent wagons. In this way a distinctive type developed that survives to this day.'

We stop next to the walking man. His name is Kiewiet Spannenberg, and he's on his way to the farm Smitskraal. 'I grew up here in the Moornaarskaroo, Meneer,' he says. 'I'm a lynx catcher. I catch them with traps and cat cages.' A tick is struggling up his trouser leg.

'A tick can smell you,' oom Fanie tells me. 'Sometimes they sommer go and wait for the sheep at the gate where they have to walk through. It comes sauntering towards you, then it bites into you and holds on. The only thing that can loosen it is pipe oil.'

11:45: The ghosts join the conversation

They say the Moordenaars Karoo is haunted. Badly haunted. Or maybe it's just that more ghost stories are told here than anywhere else in the country. This may have to do with the fact that the Moordenaars Karoo is one of the few places in South Africa that doesn't yet have any Eskom power. A supply line does run through the region, but that's to keep the new Salt telescope at Sutherland going.

There are no doubts in oom Fanie's mind. 'There are ghosts here, man,' he says, as we drive along bumpily on the R202 in the direction of Poffertjiesgat.

At Poffertjiesgat, they say, a fire occasionally breaks out on the hillside. When you get closer, it vanishes. Some people are also said to have seen a bright, bright light here on the R202 which, once it has blinded you, disappears – just like that! And sometimes at night, you can apparently hear a mournful voice calling out over the veld. They say it's a mother looking for her child that disappeared here long, long ago.

Someone who can provide first-hand evidence of the ghosts of the Moordenaars Karoo is Fielies Filander, whose story was reported in *Die Burger* in 1998. Poor Fielies. One night he was travelling through the Moordenaars Karoo on the back of his employer's bakkie, with instructions to open and close all the gates along the way. At the last gate the farmer pulled away, thinking that Fielies had already taken his seat on the back of the bakkie. (By the way, there's been a law in existence since 1912 that requires you to close a gate again after you've passed through it. If you fail to do so, you can be arrested.) But Fielies wasn't on the bakkie. He had accidentally been left behind in the pitch-dark Moordenaars Karoo, while the bakkie pushed on to Barrydale.

The next day, policemen from Laingsburg found an extremely agitated Fielies Filander next to the road, his eyes wild with fright. He told an incoherent tale about 'the most terrible unearthly noises' that he had heard in the dark.

Oom Fanie Pad has his own theory about the ghosts. 'It's just people who died in road accidents. Or drowned in the Buffels. Or who didn't die natural deaths,' he says.

He's spent many nights camped out under the stars next to his Gallion T600 road grader, but he would never stay overnight at a place like Poffertjiesgat. Oom Fanie, too, has seen that bright light on the road. He doesn't hesitate to point out the various places where people have died. Here in the Moordenaars Karoo, the dead are more present than they are in the cities. Or so it seems.

'This is where Koos Bothma crashed into one of our tip trucks and died.'

'Here at Knoffelfontein, a woman was swept away by the Buffels River and drowned.'

At a drift near Sandkraal, oom Fanie asks me to stop. 'An old man once came down there on a bicycle,' he says, and points to the steep downward slope on the opposite side of the bridge. 'He couldn't find his brakes and the front wheel got stuck in the stones at the bottom, and he flew through the air.' Oom Fanie points to a thorn tree on the river bank. 'The next day they took the guy's body out from among those branches.'

12:15: The Immorality Act

Like other places, the Moordenaars Karoo also has its secrets and tragedies, with or without bits that have been added by story-tellers over the years.

At Anysfontein, about 30 km from Laingsburg, prospectors have come searching for uranium. It seems that there are indeed radio-active substances in the region. Nico Scholtz, a researcher, wrote a thesis about this: *Assessment of Potential Toxic Influence of Uranium Trail Mining in the Karoo.* In the course of his research, Scholtz wandered around the area with a scintillation counter. 'The machine that makes the rocks scream', the local labourers called it.

We are now about 35 km from Laingsburg, oom Fanie and I. The road crosses quite a few causeways over the Buffels River. The people of the Moordenaars Karoo are occasionally cut off from the outside world when it rains – not that this is an inconvenience they have to worry about too often. The average annual rainfall is below 100 mm.

There's a small stone house on a hillside beyond Sandkraal. A tragic thing happened there, says oom Fanie, but then he clams up and refuses to elaborate.

After our trip I managed to ferret out the details by asking some other people. During the apartheid years, a young girl lived in that house. Her dad was white, her mother coloured. She was very pretty, and apparently, despite the Immorality Act that was still in force at the time, some of the young white men from the district regularly called at that little house after dark.

Then she fell pregnant. It is said that the white father of her child came to fetch her one day in a Datsun Stanza, and she was never heard of again. At least, that's how the story goes.

12:30: Phut-phut-phut...

Many old farmsteads in the Moordenaars Karoo have been abandoned and stand empty nowadays. It's a sad sight: the collapsed stone walls, the rusted windmills, car wrecks among the prickly-pear bushes, as the wind rustles by.

There are several families with the surname Bothma in the Moordenaars Karoo. But in the old days there used to be even more. To distinguish one Bothma from the other, some were given nicknames: Ryk Frikkie, Danie Rondekop, Toppie Lood.

'Oom Toppie Lood once nearly beat me up because I called him that,' oom Fanie tells me while we're crawling to the top of a rise. 'I don't have a clue why he got that nickname.'

To the right there's a farmstead that seems to show signs of life, and we drive into the yard. It's Klipbanksfontein, the home of oom Hans Simon and his wife Hettie. Oom Hans's late father, Joseph, was a Frenchman who had settled here more than sixty years ago. His late mother was Afrikaans. Yet oom Hans can't speak a word of French. He's as Afrikaans as the sun-scorched stones that are dotted around this landscape.

We stop and get out. All those years of being bounced about in a road grader have messed up oom Fanie's back and knees. 'My legs are out of focus,' he complains as we walk across the yard.

From the direction of a small room comes a sound that I haven't heard for years: 'Phut-phut-phut-phut, phut-phut-phut-phut ...'

A Lister engine.

Oom Hans has a thing about Listers. He's busy repairing about five of them in his barn at the moment. Klipbanksfontein's electricity is also supplied by a Lister that runs a generator.

It's strange: monuments have been erected to donkeys and oxen and horses in South Africa. Yet we have no monument to honour

153

the Lister engine. How many litres of water have Listers helped to pump out of our barren soil over the years?

Close to oom Hans's farm, there was once the nearest thing to a town you'd be likely to find in the Moordenaars Karoo: a tiny post office, a small school and hostel, and a little church. Services for farm workers are still held in the church, but the other buildings are in ruins.

Hettie fetches some of the old books that were used in the school. One contains an inspection report dated 1953: 'The commission requests the school board to please make the necessary arrangements with the lessors of the school for the emptying of the buckets of the newly built toilets . . .'

13:00: The fatted calf

It was a mistake: oom Fanie and I shouldn't have eaten in Laingsburg. Oom Hans has just insisted that we eat 'something small' with them for lunch.

In the Moordenaars Karoo, people consider it their duty to invite you to lunch. The 'something small' turns out to be mutton chops, rice, potatoes, pumpkin, tomatoes, lettuce. Mouth-watering country fare. And after you've already feasted on three of the tenderest of tender mutton chops, oom Hans leans forward with a fork and deposits another chop on your plate, while Hettie apologises for the absence of pudding. 'It's such a pity we didn't know you were coming,' she says. 'Then we would've cooked properly.'

After lunch, oom Hans, who also happens to be the local water diviner, gives us a short demonstration of his skills with instruments that include a saw blade and part of a fan belt. He walks across the yard, holding the blade in both hands; all of a sudden, inexplicably, it starts turning in his hands until it points straight down to a spot where there's supposed to be an underground watercourse.

It's now two hours later, and we still have goose bumps when we get back into the car. Oom Hans, a church-going man who has shunned alcohol and tobacco all his life, has just told us about the time that he drove past Poffertjiesgat early one morning when it was still dark, and saw an enormous fire breaking out against the hillside.

And when he reached the place where the fire should have been, there was nothing . . .

15:00: Back to Laingsburg

In the old days, you could drive on the R202 all the way through the Moordenaars Karoo, past Koornplaats, until you reached the Roggeveld. But nowadays the road ends about 60 km from Laingsburg, at Koornplaats, the farm of Hennie Müller.

Long ago, there was a police station and a small prison on Koornplaats, but they no longer exist. Stories are still told, however, about a certain Van der Kolk who was in charge of the station, a strict official who saw to it that law and order prevailed in these parts.

'Old Van der Kolk would just tie a stock thief's hand to the reins of his horse,' declares oom Jan Louw, who works on Hennie's farm. 'Then he'd tell the thief to run next to the horse.'

Oom Fanie and I are returning to Laingsburg on the R202, past the farm Fontein where a rusted Chev Biscayne stands in the veld. Once upon a time it rolled swankily through the streets of Laingsburg, fins shiny in the sunlight on either side of the boot, that Chev.

There are roads out of the Moordenaars Karoo that will take you to Merweville and Sutherland, but you should make quite sure that you have the right directions before venturing onto them, as signposts are rare in this region. Also, the road to Merweville is very bumpy and there are many gates to open. 'It's a subsidiary road,' says oom Fanie.

Suddenly, in the open veld, there's a rain gauge holding a supplicatory hand skywards. Empty.

We get out. Oom Fanie walks towards it on his out-of-focus legs. Across the veld, a new Land Rover comes driving in our direction.

155

The driver stops next to us and asks whether we perhaps have the GPS coordinates for a place called Klipfontein.

No, we don't, sorry.

A GPS can prevent you from getting lost here in the Moordenaars Karoo. That much is true. But a GPS won't in any way make more sense of this place.

A GPS can't tell you that the rusted Chev on Fontein once belonged to Abie Visser.

And a GPS can't tell you that nearly all the vehicle grids in the Moordenaars Karoo were built by Willem Pieterse, a proud artisan from Laingsburg.

'Don't compute time and distance,' writes the American Jim Harrison in his essay, 'Going Places'. 'Computing time and distance vitiates the benefits to be gotten from aimlessness. Leave that sort of thing to people with their categories of birthdays, average wage, height, weight, the number of steps to second floors.'

Just make two 90-degree turns, writes Harrison, and drive back on your tracks. Or stop your car and walk around a bit. Or climb a tree, or go for a swim somewhere.

This is probably the best way to travel through the Moordenaars Karoo: drive aimlessly, stop at random, talk to people. Or simply sit and allow the silence to seep into you.

Oom Fanie looks at his watch. It's already late in the afternoon. 'We must go,' he says. 'Come. Come.'

The sun is setting, and we want to get past Poffertjiesgat before dark.

The gate to Hell is wide open

She has resigned herself to living here in her little house in Prince Albert at the foot of the Swartberg, with her memories and her aching old bones. She doesn't really want to go back to Die Hel.

'Rather not, child,' says tant Susan Kellerman, 'of what use would it be?'

I sit next to her on the sagging couch in her sitting room in Vlei Street. Above our heads hangs a picture of the Voortrekker Monument. I lean towards her when I speak, because she's told me that her hearing isn't so good any more.

'Does Tante sometimes long for those days in Die Hel?' I ask.

'What did you say, child?'

'Does. Tante. Sometimes. Long for. Those days. In Die Hel.'

'It's not Die Hel, child – it's Gamkaskloof. My late pa and them got cross when people told us we came from Die Hel. Old Hennerik Mostert, a late uncle of mine, once threw away a letter from the tax people without opening it because it was addressed to H. Mostert, Die Hel, Prince Albert.'

Some people just call it the Kloof for short, that legendary valley here in the Swartberg where several families once lived, cut off from the outside world: the Mostert, Cordier and Alberts families, as well as a few others.

Many stories are told about the Gamkasklowers. Some are true. Others not.

'Is it true there was an old woman in the Kloof who could change herself into a cat, Tante?' I ask.

'You musn't come with nonsense, child. We were ordinary people, just like you.'

It is true, though, that tant Susan, who turned seventy-one in March, ran away in fear when she saw a car for the first time as a child. This was after her father, the late oom Piet Mostert, had told her one day: 'You've helped Pappie very nicely with the donkeys and the beans, my blommetjie. Pappie thinks it's now time that Pappie should show you the town.' This was when she was ten years old.

Prince Albert is the nearest town to the Kloof, which is barely 20 km long and is enfolded on either side by the Swartberg Mountains. Before the arrival of the dirt road leading to the Kloof, the journey to Prince Albert was a long, arduous slog of more than 50 km on foot over the mountains. Sometimes the Klowers arranged with someone from town to collect them once they'd reached the road.

'Me and my late pa and another old oom from the Kloof were standing at the poort at Gamka that day, waiting to be fetched,' tant Susan recalls that first encounter with the world outside the Kloof.

'Now you must remember, I'd never seen a car before, just horses and donkeys and suchlike. So I hear this thing that roars and I see a red machine coming towards us. And then I made tracks as fast as I could. I ran! The other old oom ran after me. But I thought he was also trying to get away from the red machine – and I ran even faster. Later I heard my pa shout: Come on, man! Don't be so stupid!'

As children in the Kloof, tant Susan and her cousin, also a Hendrik Mostert, once tried to enter into a pact with the devil.

'Hennerik wanted a real guitar, and I wanted a big black horse,' she relates. 'So we went to see old Daantjie Frans. He knew about witchcraft, people said. Old Daantjie told us if we gave him tobacco, he'd help us get a black horse and a guitar. Then we stole some tobacco from my pa, and that evening we went with Daantjie to the crossroads and sat there in the moonlight.

'Daantjie had a small tin guitar. He sat there going twing-twing on the guitar. This was supposed to call the devil, who would bring us a black horse and a real guitar.

'As old Daantjie was still twing-twinging like that, a cock suddenly crowed above us in the tree. What a fright we got! Hennerik just shouted: "Here's Satan!" And then we ran as fast as we could.'

Tant Susan had attended the little school in the Kloof where you could go as far as standard six. After school, she left the Kloof and came to work in a shop here in Prince Albert. She even spent some time in Cape Town, where she met her husband Johan.

She rests a hand on her chest. 'But my lungs didn't agree with the Cape, child.'

Perhaps tant Susan's lungs had spoken on behalf of her heart, because she and her new husband soon moved back to Gamkaskloof. The world outside was too full of fads and noise.

It wasn't easy to make a living in the Kloof: they toiled in the fields, in the vineyards and in the orchards. But it was a carefree life as well, especially for the children. And in the Kloof there were children in abundance – tant Susan herself is one of ten.

Then the road came. In 1962.

It was a narrow and uneven dirt road – still a good two and a half hours by car via the Swartberg Pass from Prince Albert or Oudtshoorn.

'The road into the Kloof changed everything.' Tant Susan gets to her feet with difficulty. She has food cooking on the Dover coal stove in the kitchen next door. Walking with a stoop, she goes to inspect the pots.

A short while ago, a BMW with Gauteng number plates stopped

in the street outside. A woman got out and photographed tant Susan's little house with its wide chimney, probably to show her family back home what a house and a yard from an earlier era look like. There's a chicken coop near the outside toilet, and a 1950s Chev bakkie stands next to a pile of firewood under the pepper tree.

Tant Susan returns from the kitchen and sinks down again into her hollow on the couch. 'There wasn't a life in the Kloof for us any longer after the road came, child. Nothing was the same any more.'

The Kloof had about a hundred and twenty inhabitants, but the young ones started moving away to towns and cities, and later the old ones also left – including tant Susan and her husband, who'd died in the meantime. In 1992, the last farmer sold his land to Cape Nature.

It's been years since she last visited the Kloof, which has become a popular tourist destination. 'I hear there are now thorn trees where my pa and them had their vineyards. They say it's all been destroyed.'

Sometimes strangers stop at her house and wander through the place as if it were a museum and she a museum exhibit. She is also visited by scavenging antique dealers. The other day one of them walked through the house, stopped in front of the small rosewood table in the bathroom, took out R80, gave it to her, and told her: 'I'm taking this one, my tannie.'

Another one scratched at the old sideboard, which had been hand-crafted in The Hell, to see what kind of wood it was. But this she won't sell.

She walks with me to the lopsided front gate. The little house stands apart, on the outskirts of the town. The walls need a coat of paint, the roof is rusted.

Yet the Kloof will always be here.

On the trail of Dirk Ligter

It's no use, it doesn't seem as if I'm going to find Dirk Ligter's grave here in the Woltemade Cemetery in Cape Town. Not easily.

Together with Harry de Leeuw, the administrative officer at the cemetery, I have now paged through years of grave registers in his little office among the cypresses, but we can't find the name Dirk Ligter anywhere.

Harry, with knitted brows, lowers himself again into the chair behind his desk.

'It's none of my business, Meneer,' he says. 'But is he related to you, this Dirk Ligter?'

'No,' I reply. 'He's not.'

'So, you're just looking for the grave?'

It's hard to explain. 'Once upon a time, Dirk was a famous man,' I say. 'Famous *and* infamous.'

'Was he in politics?'

'No, he used to steal sheep.'

But Dirk Ligter was not just any sheep thief. He was a legend, a man who outwitted the police at every turn. Especially in the Karoo, they still tell stories about Dirk, more than seventy years after his death – just ask around in the vicinity of Sutherland and Calvinia, and in the Ceres region.

I, too, grew up with some of those stories. When I was a kid my oom Hennie, who lived at Touws River for many years, told me how Dirk once took two baby's nappies from the farmer's washing line after he'd slaughtered a fat wether on the sly. The story goes that he sprinkled the nappies with pepper and bound them around his feet to prevent the police's bloodhounds from picking up his scent.

It was also said that old Dirk could outrun a horse, and without breaking his stride he'd take out his ramkie – his Khoi guitar – and start to sing a ditty: *'Die wit perd van Calvinie, hy loop maar hy kan nie sien nie. . .'* (The white horse of Calvinia, he walks but he cannot see . . .)

In some of oom Hennie's stories, Dirk was a sort of Robin Hood who'd give some of the meat he'd stolen to the poor.

Oom Hennie is long gone and, over the years, the Dirk Ligter stories have sunk into memory and joined all the other submerged stories of my childhood– Jakkals and Wolf, the bogeyman Antjie Somers, and CJ Langenhoven's ogres Brolloks and Bittergal. That's to say, until the other day when I came across an old edition of the writer and poet Boerneef's book *Boplaas* in an antiquarian bookshop. It contains two lovely yarns about Dirk.

'Dirk may be dead, but he lives on because he slaughtered and stole differently from the rest,' Boerneef writes in this book. 'He was an artist.'

What might the scene have been that day when Dirk Ligter was buried here in the Woltemade Cemetery? What would the minister's message have been? Were there tantes from the Karoo who sang mournful psalms, and sinewy Karoo oompies who sucked, hollow-cheeked, on a zol of Boxer or BB tobacco and gazed sorrowfully into the grave over the tips of their velskoene?

There was probably not even a minister present. All the indications are that Dirk had a pauper's funeral. The grave would have been dug, the coffin lowered, and the hole filled up by two or three municipal gravediggers.

The Lord gave and the Lord took away.

I walk from Harry's office back to my bakkie. 'You'll have to bring me a date of death,' he says. 'Otherwise our search won't lead to anything.'

When exactly did Dirk die? What *is* known, is that he died of tuberculosis in Somerset Hospital in Green Point after being brought there by Andries Kotze, a farmer from Ceres on whose land Dirk had lived at the end of his life. This would have been in the late 1920s, or perhaps the early 1930s.

But at Somerset Hospital they couldn't help me with a date. The woman at enquiries listened sympathetically when I told her how Dirk – though close to death – is said to have tried on more than one occasion to escape from the hospital with a rope made from a sheet. He wanted to return home, to the Tankwa Karoo.

'Shame,' she said, and suggested that I try the archives of the Cape Town city council. But no information was to be found there, and they in turn had directed me to the Woltemade Cemetery.

I walk among the graves on the way to my bakkie. From somewhere comes the sound of what is probably the saddest imaginable funeral music: the wind whistling through an avenue of cemetery cypresses.

It's a cold day, and the wind is driving the clouds like a herd of sheep over the interior. A teaspoon lies on a grave, and on another lies an angel with her face in the soil and a snapped-off wing, almost as if she'd executed an emergency landing on this spot.

I still remember one of the tales oom Hennie told me. As the story goes, a posse of farmers on horseback was pursuing Dirk in the Cedarberg. When at last they came close to him, Dirk darted into the midst of a troop of baboons, grabbed one by the tail, and hurled the animal towards his pursuers. The horses reared up in fright, took the bit between the teeth, and galloped away.

'Really, Oom?' I can still hear myself asking.

'Really. Your oom won't lie to you.'

One thing is sure: if Dirk does happen to be resting somewhere in this cemetery among the hundreds of unmarked graves, it's not the right place for him. He belongs among the saltbushes and the vygies of the Tankwa or the Koue Bokkeveld, and there should be stones, and a sheep bleating somewhere close by, and a high, clear sky.

Perhaps I should drive to those parts and see for myself whether Dirk's traces are still there. It's funny: the older I get, the more I travel in pursuit of words, because, so often, words are all that remain of some things – including Dirk himself, as there doesn't even seem to be a photo of him anywhere. There's no record of any children or grandchildren he might have had, because apparently the guy never took a wife.

All that's left, or so it seems, are speculations, romantic shots in the dark, and scraps of information that have assumed the nature of myths and legends over the years.

In Joe Dauth's study in his house in Kraaifontein outside Cape Town, there's a copious collection of antiques on shelves, in cupboards and on the floor: a few thousand books, stones, military uniforms, medals, photographs, maps, swords, bottles, tins, even a casket crafted by a homesick Boer prisoner of war on the island of Ceylon.

There's also a dressing gown that a woman on the passenger ship *Oceanos* was wearing when it sank off the Eastern Cape coast in 1991. (Joe, who's retired and loves to attend auctions, bought the dressing gown at one of these.)

Joe is an amateur historian who'd also grown up with Dirk Ligter stories. A few years ago, he got into his bakkie and drove into the Tankwa Karoo. He managed to track down a few people who had known Dirk, and taped the conversations he had with them. But they've all died since.

Joe hadn't been able to establish Dirk's date of death, either. 'I reckon it was in '29 or '30,' he says. 'Come and see. Come.'

In his hand is a genuine old ramkie. He talks in a whisper as he hands it to me: 'Old Dirk had one like this.'

The sound box is a BP oil can, the neck a piece of ghwarrie wood, and the bridge the brake shoe rod of a thick-wheeled Hercules bicycle. Joe was given this ramkie by the late Dirk Ambraal, a shepherd from the farm Kliphuis in the Koue Bokkeveld who had known Dirk personally.

Joe pulls a file with Dirk's name on it from a shelf. He takes out a photo of an oompie with lively eyes. 'Some people believe this is Dirk Ligter, but it isn't,' he says. 'I showed it to people who knew Dirk, and they all said it's someone else.'

This same photograph is even used in Boerneef's book, as if it's Dirk. 'The problem is,' says Joe, 'many of the stories about Dirk have had extra bits added over the years. That's what tends to happen.'

Indeed. A story is passed on from one person to another, from one generation to another, until it eventually also starts saying something about the narrators' hopes and fears.

Still, over the years Joe has managed to establish a number of things about Dirk with reasonable certainty: he was born some-where in the Tankwa Karoo around 1860. His father was a certain N. Ligter, and his mother N. Hanse. Their first names are not known.

Dirk had once been a shepherd, among other jobs he did on the farm Kleinfontein near Ceres – before he became a sheep thief. 'Some people won't agree with me,' says Joe, 'but I think Dirk started stealing sheep to punish the farmers for the injustices he felt they'd committed against his people and his friends.'

Robin Hood.

And in one particular case, Joe reckons, he even has proof of this: a charge sheet he's tracked down in the archives of the Ceres magistrate's court. Cobus Galant was sentenced to fourteen days' hard labour on 15 February 1897 because he hadn't reported for work at the farm Kleinvlei.

It is also stated on the charge sheet that, shortly afterwards,

165

Dirk Ligter slaughtered a couple of fat lambs on the farm Kleinvlei. A reprisal?

The turning point in Dirk's life must have been when he was arrested at about this time by a policeman, Albertus Nagel, and taken to the court in Ceres because he was said to have been loitering on the farm Groenfontein in the Koue Bokkeveld.

Magistrate Lorenzo Boyes found Dirk guilty and sentenced him to two weeks in jail. 'He was found wandering abroad and having no visible lawful means of support.' (People say that Dirk often worked in the magistrate's garden in Ceres when serving a short sentence.)

Joe maintains it was on that day Dirk decided enough was enough. He swore he would punish every farmer who offended him or his loved ones, by slaughtering a sheep or two.

For the next thirty, forty years, old Dirk, who was around sixty years old when he died, roamed about like a nomad and lived off the sheep he stole.

'But Dirk never, ever killed a farmer or even attempted to kill one.' Joe pushes the file back onto the shelf. 'Not once.'

He accompanies me to my bakkie.

'We have to find Dirk's grave,' he says as we say our goodbyes. 'We must re-bury him in the Tankwa.'

At Touws River, the modest railway house of my late oom Hennie and tant Bess is still here in Station Street, but the stoep no longer has the Sunbeam-red gleam it had before.

On that stoep, on a back seat that had been removed from a Ford Galaxy – or was it a Fairlane? – oom Hennie used to sit and tell stories while smoking one Gold Dollar cigarette after the other: 'On one occasion, Dirk Ligter sneaked into a farmhouse and stole the farmer's shoes. Then he put on the shoes, caught one of the sheep, slaughtered it, ate his fill, and put the shoes back inside the farmer's house. The police were totally confused.

'And you know what he did then? He gave some of the meat to the poor people.'

'Really, Oom?'

'Really. Your oom won't lie to you.'

I say goodbye to oom Hennie and antie Bess in my heart, point the bakkie's nose northwards, and take the R468 from Touws River. The road winds through mountains, past the Verkeerdevlei Dam. Gradually, the landscape becomes drier and more barren.

After roughly 40 km there's a T-junction: Ceres left, Calvinia right. I turn right. About 10 km on, to the left, is an old white house with a barn next to it. This is Karoopoort. The first main route from Cape Town to the interior – the so-called Forgotten Highway – ran past here.

In Dirk Ligter's day, this was an inn and overnight place for travellers. Dirk slept here on more than one occasion, often accompanied by a policeman, on his way to Ceres to appear on a charge of stock theft.

The house is a national monument, but the place has been vandalised. A man approaches me from the direction of an outside room. His face is so wrinkled that it resembles a road map. It's Bennie Cloete, shepherd and farm hand.

I'm half afraid to ask him about Dirk Ligter; what if he says no, he's never heard of him . . .

'Does oom know who Dirk Ligter is?' I ask, after we've finished talking about the weather and the worn-out Fiat tractor under the oak behind the house.

'Old Dirk Ligter? Do I know him? Of course I know him!'

Then he tells me one of the most famous of the Dirk stories: a constable – they say his surname was Engelbrecht – cornered Dirk here in the barren spaces of the Tankwa on a charge of sheep slaughtering, and proceeded to drive him on towards Ceres. This was the custom in those days: the prisoner had to run while the official escorted him on horseback.

Somewhere in the vicinity of Karoopoort, Engelbrecht's horse is said to have grown tired, but Dirk still had plenty of running left in his velskoene. 'Wait,' said Engelbrecht. 'Let's rest for a bit.'

'No, my duusman,' Dirk replied. 'I'm pushing on in the meantime. I'll wait at Ceres.'

In Ceres, when Engelbrecht dismounted wearily and with stiff knees from his sweat-stained horse, Dirk Ligter was sitting waiting for him in front of the police station.

Bennie doesn't know of anyone still alive who had known Dirk personally. 'Try the old people's home in Ceres,' he says. 'Old Miesies Magda van der Merwe who stays there still remembers a bit about him.'

At first there's some confusion at the Tuiste old-age home in Ceres. I knock at the gate and ask to speak to Magda van der Merwe. (She was a nurse at the Somerset Hospital at the time of Dirk's death.)

'Come with me,' offers a tannie at the gate. Then she accompanies me to a first-floor flat crammed full of photographs of children, grandchildren and great-grandchildren. A grey-haired tante opens the door. 'Tannie Magda?' I hold out my hand to her.

The tante hesitates. 'I'm Magdel, child.'

'I'm looking for tannie Mag*da* van der Merwe.'

'No, sorry, child. She's dead.'

However, tannie Magdel also knows Dirk Ligter's stories because she was married for many years to Carel, brother of Boerneef – the alias of Professor IW van der Merwe. She and her husband lived for a long time at Boplaas, the family farm of the Van der Merwes. Dirk had often visited the farm, but she never met him. He'd already died by the time she lived there.

'Go to Boplaas,' says tannie Magdel, who is eighty-nine.

I say goodbye and take the R303 from Ceres, towards Prince Alfred Hamlet, where I make another discovery: for many children in this region Dirk Ligter was a bogeyman, a kind of Antjie Somers.

'When we were naughty as kids, my mom used to threaten us and say Dirk Ligter would come and catch us,' recounts Pietman Blignault, who grew up in Prince Alfred Hamlet. 'We were very scared of Dirk Ligter.'

Yet Dirk had been dead a long time when Pietman was a child.

Beyond Prince Alfred Hamlet the road crawls up the Gydo Pass, in the direction of the Koue Bokkeveld and the Cedarberg. I stop at the top of the pass.

Sometimes, when you're travelling in pursuit of words, as I'm doing now, you wonder: is there any point in following the trail of someone who's been gone for so long?

It's all about stories, I realise a while later, as I talk to Vernon van Wyk at Op-die-berg in the Koue Bokkeveld – stories that are passed from mouth to ear, from generation to generation.

'Dirk Ligter didn't have a pa and ma,' says Vernon. 'He only had an ouma.'

Then he tells me how Dirk just had to blow on a lock, and it would open by itself.

Now I think I know why oom Hennie always told the story that Dirk used to give meat to the poor. Oom Hennie and his wife had also found it hard to make ends meet.

Maybe he just tailored the stories about Dirk to suit his own desires . . .

It's as the American writer Barry Lopez puts it: 'The stories people tell have a way of taking care of them. Sometimes a person needs a story more than food to stay alive.'

It feels as if at any moment Dirk might appear from around a corner and greet me in a way that was apparently typical of him: 'Good afternoon, my duusman. What shall I say? Where Dirk has come from, the constables are trying to find out, and where he's going, he himself doesn't even know for sure.'

A while ago I stopped here in the farmyard of Boplaas, about 80 km from Ceres. The Van der Merwes have been farming here for nine generations, since 1795. It's the only farm in the country where the entire farmyard has been declared a national monument.

The writer Boerneef grew up here, but in later years he only visited during holidays, since he was an academic in the Cape.

This region is mainly known for its fruit. Fanie van der Merwe is now the farmer, but at the moment he's occupied in his office behind the old coach house. I sit on the steps leading to the soap house – they used to boil soap here in the old days – and wait for him.

This is where Boerneef, then a young boy, saw Dirk for the first time. 'On a chilly afternoon Pa and I were sitting in the little soap house, dehusking maize, when a shadow suddenly darkened the doorway,' he writes. 'How he managed to get past the fierce farm dogs I don't know, but all of a sudden he appeared soundlessly in the doorway, just like that.'

I'm startled when Fanie unexpectedly greets me from behind. He's accompanied by his brother, Nico. They show me the Van der Merwe memorial wall they've erected, and tell me how Dirk once stole some soap.

There's a cupboard in the house where Fanie keeps, among other things, Boerneef's famous beret and his whip. Boerneef's ashes are also buried here on the farm.

I leave Boplaas with the old writer's yarns about Dirk in my mind: 'As I grew older, I started realising that Dirk was not at all such a terrifying individual.'

I drive west, in the direction of Katbakkies and other areas where Dirk used to roam. Somewhere around here, Dirk once also outran Boerneef and a certain oom Willie Ta on their horses – all the while singing them a ditty. 'Dirk has to exert himself slightly to speak, but I can't detect any exhaustion in his running,' is how Boerneef describes it.

I stop at the farm Kliphuis. Not far from the road is a white-washed, flat-roofed house. Oupa Dirk Ambraal, one of Dirk's best friends, lived here. Oupa Ambraal is also buried here.

Antjie Ambraal, one of his daughters, accompanies me to the grave in the hills. She points to a rocky koppie. 'That's the rock garden,' she says. 'Old Dirk often slept there, in the hollows.'

'Are there still people around here who play the ramkie?' I ask. 'No,' she replies. 'Nowadays, it's just the wirelesses.'

Who knows, perhaps Dirk is buried here on the farm Beukesfontein in the Tankwa Karoo.

From Boplaas I drove over the so-called Swartrug, past the breast-shaped Pramberg, which Boerneef wrote about in a well-known poem. It's a bare, cold mountain region, with piled-up rock formations that look as if they've been packed there by the gods for Dirk to sleep under.

Later the road descends via the Skittery Pass, down into the barren open spaces of the Tankwa Karoo.

When you stand here, you also get a good idea of the region where Dirk went about his business. Calvinia is more than 150 km north of here, and Dirk also went there sometimes. Some people claim that he slaughtered sheep even further north, in Bushmanland.

I've stopped here to talk to oom Jan Theunissen on the farm Beukesfontein. He tells me how Dirk would throw leopard droppings behind him to confuse the police's bloodhounds, how Dirk once saved the life of a child that had been bitten by a snake . . .

'The old folks used to say that Dirk could turn himself into an anthill or a whirlwind,' he says.

Oom Jan picks up his John Deere cap. 'Old Dirk is buried here on the farm. Or that's what my late dad used to say. Let me show you the grave.'

'Really, Oom?'

'Come.'

While the bakkie wobbles over stones as we drive into the veld, oom Jan tells me about the ninety-three lambs he has lost to jackals this year.

'Oom is probably grateful that there aren't sheep thieves like old Dirk Ligter any more,' I say.

'Not really, I actually miss the ones like old Dirk. He killed one sheep at a time. Nowadays they just pitch up in a bakkie at night and load up a whole lot. The other day I again lost eight in one go.'

Oom Jan leans forward, his voice suddenly soft: 'Stop right here.'

I walk behind him into the veld. The sun squeezes the sweat from our arms, and somewhere a dove is cooing.

Oom Jan halts abruptly. All around us are small heaps of soil and stones. Unmarked graves. Five, six of them.

Oom Jan plants his velskoen on one heap. 'I think this big one is Dirk's. I just think so.'

The other night oom Jan and his wife walked past here on their way to a trap he'd set for the jackals. 'All of a sudden I felt a kind of hot wind,' said oom Jan. 'It whirled around, that wind. In the dark.'

Who's to say Dirk Ligter didn't in fact escape from hospital with that sheet and come here to die among the fragrant Karoo bushes?

We walk among the small heaps. A whirlwind is spinning in the distance.

Dust thou art, and unto dust shalt thou return. And all that's left are the words – the words that have become stories.

And, who knows, perhaps a grave.

Idi doesn't live here any more

'And there's Cape Town,' says Bob Roberts.

He's standing on the shore of Lake Victoria just outside Kampala, the capital of Uganda, pointing to a fairly large uninhabited island about a kilometre into the lake. I ran into Bob a while ago beside the lake near Kampala, and he's not exactly friendly. But he's also not unfriendly. For some or other reason, he reminds me of the manager of a rather busy Spur restaurant.

Bob was a friend of Idi Amin, the infamous Ugandan dictator, and this was probably the attitude you had to adopt if you wanted to remain Idi's friend. When Amin ruled the country between 1971 and 1979, he had many of his 'friends' murdered, and, reportedly, even one of his wives.

His Excellency, President for Life, Field Marshal Al Hadji, Doctor Idi Amin Dada, VC, DSO, MC, Lord of the Earth and the Fishes of the Seas and Conqueror of the British Empire in Africa in general and Uganda in particular. This was the title he gave himself.

As a child I was scared of Idi Amin, even though I lived in Daniëlskuil in the Northern Cape, thousands of kilometres from here. Or perhaps scared is not the right word. For many people,

173

Idi Amin was – and maybe still is – the personification of Africa's incomprehensible, dark, even absurd and grotesque side.

Now, nearly four decades later, I'm standing here with Bob at one of Amin's former houses in Uganda. It's a double-storey house, but there's nothing extravagant about it. It looks a bit like the retirement homes that school principals and bank managers built themselves in Hermanus or Mossel Bay in the 1970s.

Near the house is a neglected oblong building with a play fountain in front. The fountain isn't playing any more. This was once a restaurant where Amin entertained guests.

Down below at the waterside lies the *Queen Victoria*, Amin's personal boat, which is completely rusted. Near the house one can still see one of Amin's beloved swimming pools. The water is dirty and filled with leaves.

Amin called the place Cape Town View because it looks out on Cape Town Island – the name given to it by Amin – which Bob has just shown me, and which Amin used as a target for mock air attacks on South Africa's Cape Town.

Bob, a businessman, apparently knew Amin well in his younger days because his father, Bob Astles, was Amin's personal pilot and adviser. When Amin fled to Libya in 1979 after a coup, it was Bob Jr who took his beloved Maserati out of the country for him.

Bob Jr has since changed his surname to Roberts, because he no longer wants to be associated with Amin.

It's almost by chance that I found my way here to Cape Town View. I was spending a few days at the Palm Beach Resort on Bugalla Island in Lake Victoria. One night, after a fiery peri-peri chicken in the thatched-roofed bar of the resort, a Ugandan barman and I chatted about Amin. How he liked to drive around the rural areas in his Maserati, even on rough two-track roads. How much Amin loved swimming. But especially how Amin, who belonged to the Kakwa tribe, had more than two hundred thousand Ugandans murdered.

Amin also shot some of the victims himself. Why? Most of them belonged to other Ugandan tribes, which he saw as a threat. He had numerous political opponents murdered, and later even some of his own ministers that he distrusted.

Then the barman told me about the island called Cape Town.

Immediately I knew what I should do. During a journey, you sometimes change your itinerary because you know this will add new meaning – or perhaps give meaning – to your journey.

I wanted to see Idi's Cape Town.

To get from Bugalla Island to Kampala, a distance of more than 300 km, I had to make use of public transport as there aren't exactly many boats on Lake Victoria. It wasn't easy, but on my first day here I had already adopted Omo's marketing slogan in Uganda as my travelling motto: *No stains, no learning*. It appears everywhere on buildings and billboards.

First I had to sail by ferry from the island to the village of Bu-kakata. Together with about four hundred Ugandans, seven old cars, and a multitude of chickens in wire cages or cardboard boxes or even just loose, with their legs tied together. (The average Ugandan chicken, you keep realising, still lives in a kind of post-Amin dicta-torship.)

From Bukakata I travelled by taxi – yes, an overloaded HiAce rattletrap, just like the ones back home in South Africa – in the direction of Kampala, to the beat of music I'd listened to as a laaitie in Daniëlskuil. The Ugandans are only just discovering the music of the seventies, it seems: the Carpenters, John Denver, Abba. You hear these oldies everywhere. 'We've Only Just Begun', 'Leaving on a Jet Plane', 'Dancing Queen' . . .

But about 60 km before Kampala – Abba's 'Waterloo' was blaring over the loudspeakers – the HiAce started jerking like a cow that had eaten too much lucerne. And came to a standstill. As dead as a dodo.

We got out. It was damn hot, and I felt impatience surging up in me. My clothes were covered in oil stains, the result of crowds on the ferry pushing me against a truck with a load of tarred poles, and everywhere around us was nothing but decay: old buildings, broken engines, emaciated dogs, litter on the pavements.

What *is* it with Africa? I wondered.

Then someone nudged me. It was one of my fellow passengers, a guy I hadn't spoken a word to. He was carrying two cold Cokes, one of which he handed to me. 'A gift for you, my friend,' he said.

Luckily, the driver and an alleged mechanic managed to get the broken-down HiAce back on the road after a lengthy struggle. The following day in Kampala I started asking around everywhere about the location of Cape Town Island. No one knew where it was.

Or perhaps they knew and didn't want to tell me, because many of the people I talked to were reluctant to discuss the Amin years. They were trying to forget that era. However, for some or other reason, several people told me how much Amin loved swimming. His favourite swimming spot was the pool at the Apollo Hotel. Today it's the Sheraton, Kampala's classiest hotel.

The swimming pool is still there, as is the strange contraption that was erected for Amin. He first had a small 'island' built in the middle of the swimming pool, a construction that was connected to land by means of a tunnel running under the pool.

Then he had a hoisting apparatus installed. At times, Idi would walk through the tunnel under the pool, climb onto the apparatus there and press a button. He'd be hoisted to the top, onto the 'island'. There he would stand, often in his swimming trunks, and address people gathered around the pool.

These days, this is just about the only monument to Idi Amin in Uganda.

In the end, a former Ugandan ambassador to Russia, whose acquaintance I'd made in the British club, explained to me where Cape Town was. ('I wish I knew why Amin never had me murdered,' he confessed after his third whiskey.)

The following morning, the third day of my search, I paid a young man about R150 to transport me on his 90 cc motorcycle –

known as a boda-boda in these parts – to Munyonyo, the area of Kampala that is adjacent to Lake Victoria.

Bob Roberts happened to be here because he'd bought Idi's old home in 2004, and intends to restore Cape Town View in order to sell it again.

Bob and I walk towards the restaurant near the house. He doesn't say a word, but as we reach the restaurant stoep he asks suddenly: 'You said you're from South Africa?'

'Yes,' I reply.

Then, as if he feels the need to confess, he tells me how Amin enjoyed entertaining people on this very stoep. The highlight of these parties would be when the MiG fighter planes of the Ugandan air force flew over and bombarded Cape Town Island, all in preparation for the major assault Amin intended launching against South Africa.

During an Organisation of African Unity (OAU) summit in 1974, Amin even invited Africa's most prominent leaders to view one of these mock attacks on Cape Town. Bob was present that day. 'There was a brass band, and lots of food and drink.' He pauses a while. 'But on that occasion none of the bombs hit Cape Town; they all missed their target and fell in the water.'

Shortly afterwards, Smuts Guweddeko, head of the Ugandan air force, was murdered.

No stains, no learning.

Bob sits on the low wall of the play fountain and lights a cigarette. He doesn't feel like any more talking.

I stand there and gaze at Cape Town, and wonder what Bob's reaction would be if I started laughing at that scared little boy from Daniëlskuil that I'd once upon a time been.

Amin died of natural causes in Saudi Arabia in 2003. South Africa was never after all invaded by Uganda.

Lo-o-ong road through the Tanqua

Oom Freddie Smal is familiar with the vagaries of the Hantam's dirt roads. 'Remember one thing, Boet,' he says, and gazes over the open veld. 'A dirt road is always different from what you think it is. Around here, for instance, you get three kinds of bends: sly bends, blind bends and stubborn bends.' He shakes his head. 'And all three of them are highly dangerous. Go carefully with them.'

Oom Freddie has been a motor mechanic here in Calvinia for many years, and has given roadside assistance to more stranded motorists than he can recall. Cars that burst through boundary fences because of stubborn bends. Cars that broke down for no reason. Cars with holes in the petrol tank, or two flat tyres simultaneously. Cars that rolled.

The R355 from Calvinia to Ceres must surely be one of South Africa's toughest roads. It's also the longest uninterrupted stretch of road between two towns in the entire country: 257 km through the Hantam, the Tankwa Karoo and the Ceres Karoo.

The Khoi people who gave the Tankwa Karoo its name either had a wry sense of humour or poor judgement. Tankwa means 'water that flows', but this region is officially the driest in South Africa.

It's a neglected part of the world. Most people who travel to Calvinia prefer to take one of the roads on either side of the Tankwa, the N7 via Vanrhynsdorp or the N1 via Matjiesfontein. They avoid the R355. Even Heinrich Lichtenstein, an itinerant botanist who trekked through these parts in 1803, was rather sceptical about the region:

> *Nowhere, as far as the eye could reach, was a tree to be seen, nor even a shrub – nowhere any signs of life, not a point upon which the eye could dwell with pleasure. The soul must rest upon the horrors of the wide-spread desert.*

But it must be added that Calvinia didn't yet exist in Lichtenstein's time. And it's a nice little town. Besides oom Freddie's workshop, it has good guesthouses, an annual meat festival, a baby competition presented by the Medchem Pharmacy, the Blou Naartjie restaurant which serves the tenderest mutton chops imaginable, an interesting museum, and even a branch of the Vrouediens that was addressed at its recent spring tea by Gené van Niekerk, the only female member of the Klipwerf boeremusiek band.

The town also has a Rolls-Royce that belongs to Dr Erwin Coetzee. It still has a real old-fashioned general store, *Mej. Dolla Parker se Winkel*. This is the name on the gable – but tant Martie Steenkamp is the person behind the counter. Miss Dolla died a few years ago, says tant Martie. So she now manages the store.

There are plastic buckets, Lennon's traditional medicine, and tennis balls on the tall shelves. On the counter, next to packets of Boxer tobacco, stands a dish with round pastries that resemble vetkoeke, just smaller and more genteel, as if customised for a town named after the old church father, John Calvin. They're called skuinskoeke, and can be found from here to Namaqualand – a safe alternative to a meat pie. Just the right padkos for the longest stretch of road in the country.

It's a good idea to buy a set of maps of the region at the offices of the surveyor general before you take on the R355. At R10 a sheet, it's a bargain.

With maps like these at your side the region isn't quite so empty any more, since they name every farm, mountain, kloof, dry riverbed and stream: Aanteelkraal, Bruinrug, Tankwafontein, Tra-tra, Papkuil. Names that are almost poetic. It's no wonder that NP van Wyk Louw, perhaps the greatest Afrikaans poet, came from these parts. He and his brother Gladstone, better known as WEG and also a poet, were born in Sutherland about 160 km from here.

I hit the road. The first stretch from Calvinia runs through the Bloukrans Mountains, down the Bloukrans Pass, round a few of oom Freddie's blind bends, and then you're in the open, liberated from cellphone reception, Quick Shops and speed traps.

'This grey-blue world instantly makes me feel different,' writes Boerneef. 'Just look at the open plains, and there, in the distance, the mountains and kloofs and crags.'

Bossiesberg. Bo-Stompiesfontein. Frans-se-dam.

The R355 isn't an excessively tough dirt road, it's just so never-ending – especially if you don't have a souped-up Ford Cortina, like Hans Matthys who works at Supa Quick in Calvinia.

The Cortina is the ideal Tankwa devourer (the more so if, like Hans's, it has an inlet valve on the bonnet that's big enough to swallow a sparrow). It's sprung just right to sweep past Eierkop and Skitterykloof at 123 km/h, all the while rocking gently, like a ship on calm waters.

Frikkie has done the journey from Calvinia to Ceres in his Cortina in 2 hours 47 minutes. 'Basically, I made the block of its engine bigger,' he divulged the formula to me earlier in Calvinia. 'Then I cut its pistons by a fiftieth and skimmed its top and put everything back again.'

It's as if the first inhabitants of this region wanted to exorcise the emptiness with names: the Hantam – the area around Calvinia – ends about 80 km outside the town. Then you're in the Tankwa Karoo, which borders on the Roggeveld in the east and the Ceres

Karoo in the south. The Tankwa Karoo and the Ceres Karoo together constitute the Onderveld, and in the middle of that somewhere lie the Springbokvlakte.

Middelput. Kromdrif. Ratelsklip.

Beyond De Bos, something quivers in a mirage far ahead in the road; later it turns into a donkey cart with a youngish guy holding the reins, a woman next to him, and a thin dog running alongside. It's hard to drive past someone on the R355. Every little bit of life helps to give meaning to the emptiness.

'Good morning, Meneer.' His name is Niklaas Louw, his wife is Miekie, the dog is Sening, and the two donkeys are Jasper and Magriet. 'We were looking for a bit of sugar, Meneer. But the people aren't there, they've gone to Porterville.'

No, he doesn't know where the bushless De Bos got its name.

'You aren't perhaps going to Elandsvlei, Meneer?' He narrows his eyes against the sun. 'I want to ask you a small favour.' Sening goes to stand in the shade under the donkey cart, an unexpected mercy. Miekie is knitting something.

'Where's Elandsvlei?' I ask.

'You just drive till you come to the sign that says Cobussegat and turn off there. When you get to Elandsvlei, please tell my brother-in-law I send greetings, Meneer. His name is Vaatjie Poggenpoel. He has a kind of black moustache and a thin beard, and he has a darkish complexion. Tell him I, Niklaas Louw, greet him in the name of the Lord. Tell him I'm sorry I don't get a chance to come and see him. I'm stuck here. I'm struggling with the sheep and the little water.'

Sening lifts his leg against the left wheel of the donkey cart.

In the Tankwa, fewer than ten farmers are still on their farms. It's the same old story as in many other farming communities: the young ones move to the city, the old ones die. The drought has also forced many farmers to sell. In the first ten months of this year the region hasn't had much more than 10 mm of rain.

This is a good area for viewing wild flowers, but because of the drought it's been a long time since the Cape marigolds and the white eendekos, the kattekruie, the kapokbossies and swaelbossies and kriedorings last bloomed abundantly, splashing their colours all over the place.

Pramberg. Die Venster. Tandskoonmaak-se-laagte.

The sign at the turn-off to Cobussegat politely but firmly instructs visitors to close the gate behind them: *Die hek sal toegemaak word, dankie.* The farmyard is about 8 km from the R355. There's no sign of Vaatjie Poggenpoel with the black moustache.

A tall man opens the front door. This is Cobus Hough, a seventh generation Hough still farming here at Elandsvlei, and owner of Cobussegat, one of five guest cottages here next to the Tra-tra River.

You've got to visit a Tankwa farmyard if you want to understand the people here better. More than anywhere else in the country, the people are in some way still pioneers, because the Tankwa has to be tamed on a day-to-day-basis. Here you still find baking ovens, attics with wooden stairs, Lister engines, coal stoves, and bucket pumps. And within walking distance of the homestead, the family cemetery.

The architecture is very different from that of a Transvaal or Free State farmyard, where all too often the homestead is a mixture of Spanish style architecture and Southfork ranch in the TV series *Dallas.*

Here things happen slowly and methodically, almost like in a Karel Schoeman novel (as a matter of fact, Schoeman's novel *Hierdie lewe* is set in the Roggeveld). First we sit down in the lounge, have a cool drink, and discuss the few millimetres of rain that fell in January. The region's average annual rainfall is 0–100 mm.

'The Tankwa's somewhere in between,' says Cobus. 'We're in the winter- as well as the summer-rainfall region. But it doesn't exactly rain here either in summer or in winter.'

He wants to show me what is supposed to be the second thick-est grapevine in the country, out in the farmyard. But on the way, there's something more interesting: Elandsvlei's old farmstead is divided in two by a wall. One half of the house has a corrugated iron roof, the other a decrepit thatched roof. That's because the boundary between his farm and that of his neighbour, Phillip Lochner, runs right through the middle of the house, with no door between the two parts.

It's something that has a long history, says Cobus, without explaining any further.

His wife Tilla brings a sheet of paper where the outline of a foot has been drawn. It accompanies a request from a farm worker who wants Cobus to bring him new shoes matching the outline, from Calvinia, the nearest place that has shops. The other day another worker came with a request of a more intimate nature. The conversation went more or less like this:

'I want to ask Meneer something. Can Meneer bring along a brassiere for my wife, please, Meneer?'

'A bra?'

'Ja, a bra, Meneer.'

'What size does she wear?'

'I don't know, Meneer. But she wears a size four shoe.'

It's not really necessary to gobble up the 257 km of the R355 with a Tankwa devourer. Take a turn-off and explore the Roggeveld and the empty spaces on either side. You will be surprised.

In these parts, believe it or not, it's possible to hire sheep, provided of course you have land to graze them on. Cobus currently hires out more than a hundred sheep, in quite a complicated transaction, because technically the hirer may sell a hired sheep as long as he returns a similar one to the owner in the end.

Beyond Cobussegat is a signpost: Tankwa Karoo National Park. This road also takes you to Middelpos and Sutherland, via the scenic Oubergpas. I turn off there.

The park extends over 80 000 ha, but there are few amenities. The Tanqua Guesthouse is nearby, however, and it even boasts a landing strip (though it could probably be argued that the entire Onderveld is a landing strip).

If you don't have a surveyor's map, you should at least have a good road map because many road signs seem also to have withered in the drought.

Suddenly there's action in the rear-view mirror: a cloud of dust is pushing a bakkie across the veld. It's the first sign of traffic since Niklaas's donkey cart this morning. Lewis Stores, it says on the door of the bakkie. The driver waves and shoots past me. On the back is what looks like the new Savanna couch (R195 over 12 months).

Windheuwel. Boonste Jakkalshok. Diepgat.

Middelpos is a place you really should spend a day at, even if you just sit in the bar and drink the whiskey that's poured for you by one of the oldest barmen on the planet.

Middelpos is actually a farm, but in 1873 a man called Tomlinson built a shop here. Later the post office, the houses, the police station and the hotel followed – and recently also trouble, because there's been friction about municipal services between Koos van der Westhuizen, the present owner of the farm, and the approximately three hundred and forty people living there.

Seated on a slatted bench on the stoep of the hotel is the barman, 86-year-old oom Boeta Henke. It's now just past one in the afternoon, and apart from a rather half-hearted whirlwind near the police station, there's not much movement here. It feels as if John Wayne might come riding down the main street on his horse at any moment.

'I'm sitting here,' says oom Boeta, 'because they're in my room.' He doesn't say who they are.

Oom Boeta is not Middelpos's most illustrious resident. That would be Professor Black – Professor Dr Robert Black, QC, FRSA, FRSE, professor of law at the University of Edinburgh in Scotland, who is known in particular for his involvement in the trial of the Libyan terrorists responsible for the 1988 Lockerbie air disaster in Scotland. These days he lives at Middelpos for five months of the year, but at present he's in Scotland.

Sir Anthony Sher, the famous actor and writer who chose to be-

184

come a Brit, also has connections with Middelpos. He even wrote a novel, *Middlepost,* which is based on the life of his grandfather, a Jewish itinerant trader, who also owned the place once upon a time.

Middelpos also once had a formidable tug-of-war team, says Koos van der Westhuizen, a friendly man.

It's still a real old hotel with shiny floors and a lounge, a new dartboard, and a mass grave near the back door where a bunch of British soldiers were buried. Koos brings a container filled with worn cartridge shells, rusted nails, bits of wood, and a ruined mouth organ, items that he picked up at a place nearby where Boer forces under the command of General JL van Deventer attacked a British convoy in 1902 and set their ammunition wagons alight – the biggest explosion in the history of Middelpos.

The other day Koos went looking for more fragments, but suddenly he couldn't find anything. He suspects that the ostriches have gobbled up the last remains of the Battle of Middelpos.

Oom Boet enters the bar again, but is dead against the idea of being photographed behind the counter. 'No photos,' he says. 'No, no, no.'

'Oom Boetatjie is a bit upset,' explains Helena, Koos's wife. 'This morning they moved the furniture in his room.'

The Van der Westhuizens invite you to have lunch with them, as is customary in these parts. But it's still 80 km to Sutherland, and there are dark clouds on the horizon.

'At least take a sweet potato with you,' says tant Martie Wright, Koos's mother-in-law, and holds the dish out to me.

Sutherland is 110 km from Matjiesfontein and about 240 km from Ceres. And 1 277 400 000 km from the planet Saturn.

In the main street, near the Karoo Hotel, there is a cemented pile of stones on the sidewalk with a copper plate depicting the earth and Saturn in their orbits, with the distance between the two planets provided as well. A kind of interplanetary road sign.

Sutherland is abuzz nowadays. A few years ago you could still buy a lovely old stone house here for R60 000. These days there's nothing to be had under R250 000. There are guesthouses, the Louwhuis Museum, a restaurant, the Halley-sê-kom-eet coffee shop, a stock car club, and a cheese factory where, among the more usual sorts, you will find sheep's milk cheese. *Sheep's* milk cheese.

One name is whispered everywhere: Mark Shuttleworth.

A rumour that Mark was going to buy the Karoo Hotel had the town all agog a year or so ago. Other rumours abound, too: Mark is going to build a lodge here. Mark is going to have the road to the new Salt telescope tarred, out of his own pocket.

'But the sale fell through,' says Anette Visser, manager of the Karoo Hotel. Besides, it seems that it wasn't really Mark who wanted to buy the place, but someone connected to him.

Anette is standing in the bar of the Karoo Hotel, probably the only establishment of its kind south of Saturn where the local Dutch Reformed Church calendar hangs behind the counter. She looks at me, there's a pause, then she looks at the barmaid, and says: 'Should we give him the Merino?'

I get the Merino Suite on the top floor of the Karoo Hotel.

Actually, it's not entirely true that Sutherland owes its revival to rumours about Mark Shuttleworth, says Jurg Wagener, estate agent and owner of Halley-sê-kom-eet. The building of the new telescope has also contributed to the town's growth, as has an article in a property magazine.

It's said, too, that the actor Tobie Cronjé was recently here.

Some people also visit Sutherland because it's the coldest place in the country and they want to experience it for themselves. (If you want to know why it's the coldest place, just don't ask a guy called Seun Grobler after ten at night in the bar of the Karoo to explain it to you. You're likely to be even more climatologically confused afterwards.)

The Louwhuis – the house where poets NP van Wyk and WEG Louw grew up – is worth a visit, particularly when the guide is

Letitia Appolus. She even knows where the gin bottle on the one table comes from. Apparently the poet DJ Opperman gave it to NP.

One room in the house is dedicated to Sir Henry Olivier, a famous dam engineer and native of the town who was involved in the building of the Gariep, the Kariba and the Cahora Bassa – a fitting occupation for someone from such a dry region.

In the corner of a back room, a bust of Mr Adriaan Vlok, minister of law and order in the previous dispensation, is hidden behind some other objects. He hailed from Sutherland.

Water is constantly on everyone's mind. In front of the Karoo Hotel, at the petrol pumps, in Ettiene Viviers' shop and at the bottle store, everywhere you see people who keep glancing at the clouds in the distance.

Two little girls come running up to me in the street: 'Oom, we're collecting money. Won't Oom please buy a raffle ticket from us, Oom?'

'What are you going to do with the money?'

'We want to go to the aquarium, Oom. In Cape Town, Oom.'

The sun is low on the horizon and it's now time to buy a bottle of kambro jam, take your skuinskoeke, and drive to a hill outside the town where you sit and eat while watching how Van Wyk Louw's poem about a summer evening in a Karoo town comes to life, down to the copper-coloured twilight he mentions.

And then it starts raining.

The clouds have been holding back for more than a day, but then a warmish wind begins blowing and the first drops fall.

I leave the hotel early in the morning, going back to the Tankwa, back to the R355 to complete that stretch of 257 km between Calvinia and Ceres. Today there's more activity on the R355: some sopping-wet road workers are standing in the road, inspecting the one front wheel of their minibus.

'It's flat,' says Theo Johnstone, their leader. 'If you could please go and tell baas Jan Theunissen on the next farm he should please phone Ceres and tell them we lost a wheel.'

At Beukesfontein oom Jan peers over the lower half of the door, also wet, because he's just been checking how much water has been collected in the rain gauge in the yard.

'It now stands at 2 mm,' he says, and excuses himself because the telephone has started ringing. The call is from a neighbour. 'I've had two so far, and you?' are oom Jan's first words.

A kettle is singing on the coal stove in the kitchen and the walls are covered with photographs of children and grandchildren who are all somewhere far from here. Oom Jan comes back and sits down again. The droughts and heat and hardship have left their marks on his face. In the past four years here at Beukesfontein, he's killed ninety-seven jackal that attacked his sheep.

The telephone rings once more and oom Jan goes to answer it. This time it's a relative who also farms nearby. 'I've just had a look,' says oom Jan. 'It's almost two . . . Ja . . . Ja . . . Good heavens, ja, we really need it . . . Ja, ja, the Lord has been good to us . . . No, no, the sheep will just have to get wet . . . I say: they just have to get wet! Ja . . . Ja . . .'

Here it doesn't rain 7 or 8 mm. It rains 1 mm + 1 mm + 1 mm + 1 mm + 1 mm + 1 mm, while the phones ring repeatedly and the kettle boils and the sheep get wet and the water starts flowing in the road.

Kleinpootsrivier, Soutpansrivier, Wolfsrivier. The dry beds all suddenly have a trickle of water.

Knegsbank. Ramkop. Vryery.

This section of road is part of the Forgotten Highway – the main route between the Cape and the north until the late 1800s. It winds its way stubbornly between the Witteberge, up to Karoopoort, where an old white house with an attic and an avenue of fig trees stands next to the road.

It's actually an old inn, a national monument, and a young man and a big brown dog are standing at the gate. 'Does he bite?' I point to the dog.

'Not during the day, Meneer. He only bites at night.'

The Herberg in Karoopoort is a good last stop before you complete the final 40 km of the R355. Unfortunately the place is now closed, but you can still take a walk in the yard.

The inn was built around 1850 and served as a stop over for transport drivers, trekboers and adventurers. The building is on state-owned land, and until 1950 the lease stipulated that the tenants were required to provide overnight accommodation to any traveller who requested it.

The longer you drive around here, the more you become aware of the old truth that the real pleasure of a journey lies in the finer details of a region: in Vaatjie Poggenpoel and in hired sheep, in 86-year-old barmen and skuinskoeke, in Beukesfontein's rain gauge, in the Karoo Hotel's Merino Suite and Adriaan Vlok's half-hidden bust, in kambro jam and in the whirlwinds that twirl across the plains like restless spirits. That's why people make a mistake when they avoid the R355 out of fear of Lichtenstein's 'horrors of the wide-spread desert'.

Bobbejaanput, Ghwaapberg, Kalkgat-Oos, Langhuis, Jan-Swart-se-berg, Kompromis, Voorsteléplek . . .

Yes, the R355 is a long road. Though still hopelessly too short.

The heart of the Bushveld

It sounds as if oom Koekies Engelbrecht of the Deo Gloria roadside stall near Brits knows exactly where the Bushveld is. Just drive north, he directs me, past Brits, past Beestekraal, till you get to Assen. You'll see a flat stretch of rock there. That's where the Bushveld officially starts.

But I wonder: is this area around Brits not already the Bushveld? After all, you find marula trees and rosyntjie bushes here. And men in khaki clothes. And a lot of butcheries.

It's strange. All the other well-known regions in the country – the Little Karoo, the Camdeboo, the Hantam, the Richtersveld and Namaqualand – are clearly shown in atlases and on road maps. But not the Bushveld, for some or other reason.

About one aspect, however, everyone agrees: the Bushveld lies somewhere in the north of the old Transvaal. That why I'm now driving northwards on the R511, through Brits, in the direction of Thabazimbi, because I'm looking for the true Bushveld – *and* true Bushvelders. And one thing is sure, when you think of the Bushveld, you think of more than just a geographical region. You think of old Jan van Till, the Bosveldbul, who brushes his teeth with chlorophyll; and of kudu horns mounted on stoep walls and mampoer and hunting rifles, biltong, cholesterol and anxious antelopes.

In an essay that appeared in 1950, Fritz Steyn, one of the few Afrikaans Bushveld writers, describes the typical Bushvelder as follows:

> *Just knowing that a kudu has been shot on your land in living memory is a wonderful thought that turns every Bushvelder into a pioneer, and the simple fact that one can still shoot a kudu or an impala on one's own land is of greater cultural significance than any outsider would ever realise. This immediately turns the farmer into a voortrekker. He is hospitable, his rifle is a shrine in the house, and he is generous with his money. They are fine people, such brave, open-hearted, living reminders of the good old days!*

Of course, but the question remains: is life in the Bushveld still like this?

Searching for the Bushveld is a bit like conversion: at some point you just know for sure that you've found it. And then, after a while, you begin to doubt again.

North of Brits the vegetation becomes more and more lush. There are rocky hills and grey louries in the trees, and all sorts of posters on the telephone poles: Jack Russell puppies for sale. Boerbulls for sale. Archery. Diesel pumps.

Then, around a bend, there's another roadside stall: Ron's Bosveld Biltong.

Maybe *this* is the unofficial southern gateway to the Bushveld, I decide, because at Ron's you can buy seventeen different kinds of game biltong – or at least that's what it says on the signboard on the roof. Also, the man behind the counter has a solid Bushveld name: Seun. Seun Moleko.

Seun is involved in a heated discussion with a man dressed in khaki. 'Are you telling me you've got bugger-all biltong?' shouts the man, and walks back to his bakkie.

I go up to him. Surely someone who's so passionate about biltong would know where the boundaries of the Bushveld are. He introduces himself as Seef Gerber, but of course I call him oom – it's Bushveld etiquette: call everyone oom who looks more than ten years older than you, or who carries more than three pens in his breast pocket.

'No, no, this is amateur Bushveld,' says oom Seef. 'The real Bushveld starts at Thabazimbi.' But he hasn't yet finished with Seun. He approaches him again. 'These seventeen kinds of game biltong of yours,' he says. 'Tell me what they are! Come on.'

'Kudu, impala, blesbok . . .' Seun excuses himself and consults a man who is slouching against a pole. Then he returns and says: 'We've got eland, too.'

Oom Seef is a Bushveld professor – a professional hunter. Or a 'pee aitch', as they are respectfully called in these parts.

From oom Seef I learn two other important bits of Bushveld etiquette. First, never brag about a kudu you've shot if its horns are shorter than fifty inches. And second, never admit that you've had too much to drink. 'Just say you've been over-served,' he advises.

Not far from Ron's, there's a signboard: *Fyndraai*. This is an angling resort, here in the amateur Bushveld, with a few huts and a girl named Annatjie van Schalkwyk who calls you oom.

'Oom can't fish here now,' she says. 'It's too dry.'

'Where does the name come from?' I point to the sign at the gate.

'From my mom, Oom.'

'From your mom? How did that happen?'

'She rolled our car on one of the fine bends around here, Oom.'

At Assen I turn off the R511, past oom Koekies's imaginary Bushveld boundary, and travel on a dirt road to Rooiberg. From there I drive through spectacular mountains to the Marekele National Park, about 10 km from Thabazimbi.

Now I know for sure that I'm in the Bushveld: near the Marekele caravan park a man comes walking towards me in the road, a squirrel on his shoulder. Meet Pottie Potgieter and Flippie.

Fritz Steyn warned as far back as 1950 that one shouldn't stereotype the Bushvelders. All sorts of people live in the Bushveld, and not all the men wear khaki. And the women don't all look as if they're on their way to a recording of *Noot vir Noot*. Some Bushvelders are really ordinary. Some are rich and drive big 4x4s, others are poor and travel on the back of those 4x4s.

Take Pottie, for instance. He doesn't wear shirts. He's the closest thing to a hippie you'd find in the Bushveld, even though it stands to reason that he's not a vegetarian. Also, he listens to Dozi rather than Bob Dylan. Pottie is a signwriter, and it's been seven years since he first unhitched his caravan at this spot.

And he's still here. 'You're free here,' he says. 'I even go to the bank without a shirt.' He leans closer, as if he wants to share the Bushveld's biggest secret with me. 'The Bushveld climate is excellent for signwriting. There's just the right amount of moisture in the air.'

It's early evening, 15 km outside Thabazimbi. Francois du Toit, a teacher at the Frikkie Meyer high school, who listens to Leonard Cohen's latest CD in his bakkie and talks about Eugène Marais, is taking me to the best firefly-viewing site in the Bushveld.

We stop on Bakkers Pass. Kransberg, one of the highest peaks in the Waterberg, stands like an exclamation mark against the moonlight. Somewhere a jackal (or melancholy farm dog) is howling, while the bush whispers all kinds of primeval secrets to something deep inside you; and then, later, when the beers have been opened, the fireflies light their lamps and perform fly-pasts for us.

The next morning I discover that I wasn't in the Bushveld after all. Or perhaps I was in the Bushveld yesterday, but somewhere between Thabazimbi and Rankins Pass I seem to have crossed some or other imaginary boundary, because Inspector Johan

Grundlingh, commander of the police station here at Rankins Pass, denies vehemently that this is the Bushveld.

'This is the Waterberg,' he says firmly. 'The Bushveld starts other side Sandrivierpoort, this side of Vaalwater.' He smiles wryly at me. 'Here things aren't what they seem, they're different.' Indeed.

Rankins Pass, about 70 km west of Thabazimbi, is a little place with a shop, a police station, fifty postboxes and a few houses. But there's no mountain pass here. The pass is some distance away.

There's surely no one who's made the Bushveld – and the Waterberg in particular – as famous as writer and naturalist Eugène Marais, has done. It was during his stay of about eight years with oom Gys and tant Maria van Rooyen on the farm Rietfontein near Naboomspruit, that Marais did most of the research for his best-known books: *The Soul of the White Ant*, *My Friends the Baboons* and *Dwaalstories*.

To get to Rietfontein, you drive further east from Rankins Pass, on a dirt road past Alma, where an advertisement for 'poodle pups with the most beautiful little champagne ears' is stuck to the wall of the shop. There's also a photostat of a photo of a team of fencers, with a message below it that highlights their competitive advantage: 'This team can work independently.'

Rietfontein is now a holiday resort. But many of the descendants of the late oom Gys and tant Maria still live around here. One of them is oom Loffie van Emmenes, a grandson of oom Hans (Purekrans) van Rooyen, who was also a close friend of Eugène Marais.

Oom Loffie, who farms near Palala, is one of those brave, open-hearted farmers Fritz Steyn wrote about. He talks about the Boer War as if it happened yesterday. Oom Loffie is still upset about a TV programme a few years ago which alleged that Marais's suicide near Pretoria happened partly because of the Bushvelders' rejection of him and his morphine addiction.

'That's nonsense, man,' he says. 'My grandpa personally sent someone to Naboomspruit with a horse cart to go and pick up

Marais on the day he committed suicide, because Marais wanted to come back to the Bushveld.' He shakes his head. 'We Bushvelders are hospitable people.'

That's true. I already have a bag of wood and two plastic bags filled with biltong in the car, and at the petrol pumps in Marken, Karel Delport gives me a lo-o-ng story as a present. In a nutshell, it's about how a lion chased him on a railway line, and how he pulled the signal and shunted the lion, which was hot on his heels, to Musina.

The Bushveld is full of stories and legends. Oom Loffie van Emmenes tells how General Jan Smuts left his binoculars behind on Khruwane, another high Waterberg peak. However, in Nylstroom, now known as Modimolle, Johan Steyn tells me, no, General Smuts left the binoculars on Kranskop.

This much is true: Kranskop, a pyramid-shaped mountain in the veld this side of Modimolle, helped to inspire the design of the Voortrekker Monument near Pretoria. Gerard Moerdijk, the architect of the monument, had a farm close by. It is said that Kranskop was also in Marais's mind when he wrote his famous short story 'Salas y Gomez'.

I'm now on the road heading further north, past Villa Nora to Ellisras. Ellisras is undiluted Bushveld. Bosveld 'unplugged'. You know this instinctively when, seated in Neels Taute's bar at the friendly Bundu Inn guesthouse, you hear oom Piet Erasmus, a former Bushveld detective, shout at the TV showing some or other *National Geographic* programme: 'Do you guys see that bush pig! I've eaten one of those!'

It's late afternoon, and Ben Harmse and his girlfriend Maja Oosthuizen – both professional hunters – are sitting in Jan se Gat, a bush camp outside Ellisras, together with Jan Eckhard, the owner, and a certain Petoors, another practising Bushveld professor.

They drink Old Brown sherry and tell hunting stories. Two years ago, Ben ate two hundred and fifty earthworms at the Bushveld show here in Ellisras, setting a new unofficial world record for eating earthworms. Ben is also the first guy in South Africa to have succeeded in shooting the Big Five with a crossbow.

'I stopped counting a long time ago how many buffaloes I've shot,' says Ben.

The sun is setting, there are birds in the tree above us, and around us the Bushveld lies peaceful and still. 'But there are three animals that I won't ever shoot: a bushbaby, a bat-eared fox and a giraffe.'

'And what if an overseas hunter offers you a lot of money to take him on a giraffe-shooting expedition?' I ask.

'Then I let Petoors go with him,' replies Ben.

This search for the Bushveld is turning into a nostalgic journey. Everywhere, the typical old Bushveld way of life – despite all the brave, open-hearted people – is disappearing. More and more rich businessmen are buying up farms, closing them off with game-proof fences, giving the places pretentious names, building Lost City-type lodges, and trying to lure as many overseas hunters as possible to the area.

As Neels Taute puts it: 'The easiest way to spot the foreigners here in Ellisras is to look for people wearing brand-new khaki clothes.'

Apparently even a prince from Saudi Arabia recently bought four farms next to the Limpopo River. Ellisras already has a Shoprite and a Spar – and the Boeppens Biltong Bar. That's why I feel rather wistful as I stop in front of the Hennie de Lange café and cash store at Steenbokpan, a fifty-postbox dorp west of Ellisras. All over the Bushveld, from Vier-en-twintig-riviere to Palala and Beauty, you see the ruins of shops like this.

A tante stands behind the counter of the Hennie de Lange café.

'Is oom Hennie here?' I ask.

'I'm Hennie,' she replies. 'But if you want to speak to oom Hennie, he's next door at the shop.'

They are brother and sister, both were born here in Steenbokpan, and both were baptised Hendrik Jacobus de Lange. Tant Hennie was the seventh of a string of daughters, so her father, old oom

Hennie, gave up hoping for a son and named her after himself. And then, can you believe it, a boy was born. So he was named Hendrik Jacobus as well.

Oom Hennie's cash store is still an authentic old-time store that smells of paraffin and soap and brown sugar; with rolls of fabric and shoe boxes on tall shelves against the wall, and bicycle tyres and spades hanging from the ceiling. And amidst all of this sits oom Hennie, with piles of papers and an old pair of pliers on a table in front of him.

'As far as I'm concerned,' he says, 'this is the only Bushveld. How can you hunt where there are mountains? Hunting is done on flat land.'

Oom Hans Engelbrecht, tant Hennie's husband, also helps in the shop. Before long, tant Hennie arrives with a plate of pap and frikkadels for each of us, which we're going eat right there in the shop. But first we have to say grace. 'Ogies!' oom Hennie shouts loudly. And everyone in the shop – customers included – closes their eyes.

'Go and visit the Ox brothers if you really want to know what the old Bushveld was like,' said oom Piet Erasmus, the detective, while he was earlier tucking into a Blue Bull steak in Neels's bar.

The Ox brothers' surname is actually De Beer – oom Rusty and oom Hendrik de Beer – and their farm near Monte Christo borders on the Limpopo River. They're called the Ox brothers in these parts because they never married. Ever since their mother's death, oom Rusty and oom Hendrik, seventy-four and seventy-eight years old respectively, have lived alone on the farm. Just like in the olden days. Without electricity or any other modern conveniences.

'The Bushveld isn't a place,' mumbles oom Hendrik. 'The Bushveld is in your heart.' And then, out of the blue, he starts reciting an old poem by Jan F Cilliers where the Bushveld is mentioned.

The prince from Saudi Arabia also came to have a look at their farm. 'The guy was here in a Mercedes 4x4,' says oom Rusty, 'but his wife didn't even get out of the car. And, would you believe it, he actually wore khaki clothes.'

'The last time I was in Pretoria, I was struck by lightning,' oom Willie chips in. 'I was carrying a pole on my shoulder, and the lightning hit the pole.' Oom Willie points to his right shoulder. 'Then the bolt went through the pole, through my stomach, right down into my left leg.'

'When was that, Oom?'

'In nineteen hundred and eighty-two.'

Oom Hendrik de Beer is probably right: the Bushveld lies in the heart of individuals, because by now I've travelled nearly 1 400 km through the north, from Pretoria to Ellisras, then up to the Limpopo River and past Swartwater and Maasstroom, up to Alldays, and I still don't know exactly where the boundaries of the Bushveld lie.

Just when I think I know, someone says no, this isn't the real Bushveld, the real one is actually over there. And I haven't even been behind the Soutpansberg, to Phalaborwa, Bela-Bela, or in the Marico.

The Afrikaans writer and storyteller Pieter Pieterse has described this phenomenon rather romantically. In one of his sketches he writes: 'Today I know: everyone's Bushveld is different. Perhaps there are mopani trees and raasblaar trees and fish eagles in *your* Bushveld. Perhaps not. Or maybe there's a jackal that howls every night at dusk.'

But wherever your Bushveld may be, you'd probably find pee aitches there. And good signwriting weather. And bush. And a mountainside where General Smuts's binoculars may be lying. And anxious antelopes. And friendly people. And stories – above all, stories.

Being where you are

If all goes well, I should be with oom Albertus Bam in Rooibank
by about two o'clock this afternoon, I reckon, as I take the C14
beyond Rietoog and head west. Towards the desert. To the Namib.

Oom Albertus will hopefully not be too ill to tell stories. Maybe
a fire will be burning in his Dover stove, and maybe he'll have regained enough strength to make us coffee – strong Kloof coffee in
those green packets. Then we'll sit in front of his modest house,
he and I, and the Namib will be peaceful and lovely.

Maybe I can even spend the night there at Rooibank.

I glance at the worn-out road map of Namibia – already doing its
fifth trip to these parts – lying next to me on the seat of the Golf
Chico. Rooibank is still about 300 km away, north, in the direction
of Walvis Bay.

I open the window and turn up the volume of the Johnny Clegg
cassette in the tape deck. 'The world is full of strange behaviour,
every man has to be his own saviour,' sings Johnny, while the Namib unfolds in all its splendour outside the Chico. To the south lie
the Tsaris Mountains; to the west the Nauklauf, with its shadows

and rough spine. Over there in the distance, beyond Remhoogte, the dunes draw a thin red line across the horizon.

Saagberg, Nuwedam, Guisis, Abasis – I know the names of many of these mountains, ravines and places, because I keep on returning to the Namib.

Nauchas. Sukses. Sesriem. Middelpos. Zaris.

This time, my decision to come was taken on the spur of the moment. My friend Christo visited the Namib recently, and I'd asked him to please drop in, if possible, on oom Albertus at Rooibank and give him my regards. And then Christo phoned the other night. He did go and see oom Albertus, he said, and the old boy was very ill.

We go far back, oom Albertus and I. Over the years he has taught me much about the desert. He was born here eighty-nine years ago and is as much part of the Namib as the sand, the wind and the silence. I can't imagine coming to the Namib without calling on him and listening to his wise stories.

After the conversation with Christo, I sat there on my sofa, and all of a sudden I didn't want to be in Pretoria. I wanted to be in the Namib rather than here among all the people and the intrigues, the cars, the lights and the barking dogs. I wanted to sit on my backside on the sand in the late afternoon somewhere in the open spaces between Spreetshoogte and Aruvlei, and let the silence seep into me. I wanted to drink Kloof coffee again with oom Albertus at Rooibank.

Sometimes you just get the urge to escape to a place where, you believe, you can once again become the person you feel you should be.

The following day I applied for leave and booked an air ticket, and yesterday I flew to Windhoek and hired the Chico at the airport. It's the only rental car I can afford, but I reckon you can get from here to Rooibank in a Chico – a Chico and faith and hope and a towrope, just in case you get stuck somewhere or the car breaks down.

It would have been easier to drive on tar all the way from Wind-hoek via Okahandja and Usakos to Swakopmund and Walvis Bay in the Namib. Rooibank is only about 40 km from Walvis Bay, next to the dry riverbed of the Kuiseb.

But I prefer approaching the desert from the south. Sometimes it feels to me as if Swakop and Walvis are not really part of the Namib any more. In Swakop there's a casino, a Spur, beauty salons, a karate club; and at Langstraat, between Swakop and Walvis Bay, busloads of tourists nowadays pose in front of the Burning Shore Guest House, where Brad Pitt and Angelina Jolie stayed when they were here for the birth of little Shiloh Nouvel Jolie-Pitt.

When you drive into the Namib from the direction of Rehoboth and Rietoog, it's as if the landscape prepares you for the barrenness and emptiness to come: first the trees become smaller and sparser, then there's just bushes and grass. And later, just grass. Still later, there's not even grass, only stones. Then, somewhere beyond Ababis, the stones run out as well and the first dunes appear.

Whenever I drive into the Namib, it feels as if I'm driving into a quiet place somewhere inside myself.

A splash of green is visible in the distance. Later the splash be-comes trees and buildings, a water tank, a satellite dish and a phut-phut-phutting Lister engine.

This is Solitaire.

I always stop here, even if it's just to eat a chunk of shop manager Moose MacGregor's apfelstrudel. The last time I was here, about four years ago, Moose and I sat for a long time on the stoep of the shop drinking one Mirinda cool drink after the other, because the other drinks were all sold out.

I remember how Moose, with Zen-like calm, killed four flies with the flat of his hand that day.

Solitaire is changing.

There's a lodge here now, and next to the shop is a pub with a lean-to in front of it. At the two petrol pumps, cars are waiting in line to have their tanks filled.

The only parking space I can find is some distance away. I get out of the car and walk towards the shop. The small stone kraal that used to house a puff adder is gone.

On the stoep of the shop, people are clustered around the tables: Germans, Hollanders, Spaniards, South Africans, and a guy who looks as if he might once have been a member of The Village People band. He's dressed in a khaki shirt, cycling shorts and a purple Stetson that seems slightly luminescent.

At least Moose is still here, I'm immediately aware; there's a generous wedge of his renowned apfelstrudel on the plate of almost every person sitting on the stoep.

It might sound unlikely, but Moose's apfelstrudel is still partly responsible for the bustle here at Solitaire. He began baking apfelstrudel a few years ago, mainly because it requires few ingredients.

One day a journalist arrived, wrote an article about his apfelstrudel experience, and people started visiting Solitaire to experience it for themselves. More articles followed, in international magazines, too, and more and more people flocked here. Now they get so many visitors that it sounds as if Moose is losing his head.

'Fifteen minutes!' roars a voice inside the shop.

I enter and see Moose scurrying to and fro behind the counter. The apfelstrudel is sold out, and the next batch will only be ready in a quarter of an hour. 'Fifteen minutes!' he roars again in the direction of a small group of slightly startled Dutch tourists.

The Village People man with his luminous Stetson positions himself squarely in front of Moose. He speaks English with a European accent. 'I vant some longk-life milk,' he says.

A wildish gleam appears in Moose's eyes. 'No long-life milk,' he replies. 'No long-life milk.'

'Not-ting?'

'Nothing.'

'Vhen vill you get?'

'I don't know!' roars Moose and flings his arms into the air, as if he's surrendering. 'It's the Chinese! They're buying up all the world's bloody long-life milk! Millions and millions of litres! They're taking over the bloody world, the Chinese!'

Moose would definitely not be able to kill four flies with Zen-like calm this morning.

He and his wife moved here from Cape Town about ten years ago to manage the shop. But after eight months she returned to the Cape. They were divorced subsequently, and Moose is still here.

I go to talk to him, but he seems not to remember me. He also knows nothing about oom Albertus Bam.

'What happened to the puff adder, Moose?' I ask.

'Some mad oke killed it with a stone.'

'Why?'

'I told you, he was koekoes.'

I return to the stoep, sit down at a table, and from my camera bag I take a book that I'm rereading for the third time: Bruce Chatwin's *The Songlines*.

Chatwin, a British travel writer who died far too young, understood better than anyone this urge that sometimes compels one to go and retrieve a part of oneself in a far-off place. 'I was forced to travel, to ward off the apparitions assembled in my brain,' he writes.

At the table next to me sits a guy with an army bush hat. He's moving a bottle of Tafel Lager in endless circles around his car keys in front of him. He nods in my direction. He feels like talking.

'Is that your blue Chico?' he asks.

I nod, and attempt to refocus my attention on the book.

Solitaire may be a tiny place, but it has inspired the formation of a society: The New Age Society of Solitaire. They even have a website where they express thoughts such as: We are multidimensional beings currently having a human experience.

Some of the members apparently come here at times to meditate and to talk about Zen Buddhism and other spiritual matters.

I order a Tafel from the waiter and try to avoid a conversation with the guy wearing the bush hat next to me. I just want to sit here and read and let the desert filter into my senses.

In the city, your senses are constantly bombarded by things. In time they become so blunted that you no longer see, hear, taste or feel anything. In the desert you become aware again of what is around you, because there's so little of everything here. That's why a desert is a spiritual place, writes Chatwin.

A bird flies over the roof of Moose's shop. It looks like a mossie. It *is* a mossie. A mossie is a highly underrated flier. Just watch carefully the next time you see one flying. The mossie flaps its wings, rocking to and fro in the air, and makes a landing near the tickey-box.

Solitaire is no longer the same.

The sound of testosterone rings out over the veld as two quad bikes race towards us in a cloud of dust. From somewhere comes the sound of a saccharine trumpet that sounds disconcertingly like Kenny G.

There's still a queue of cars at the petrol pumps. It's easy to distinguish between a South African and an overseas tourist at a petrol pump: the South African guy usually slides out from behind the wheel, contentedly stretches, and wiggles his pants loose from between his buttocks – completely unembarrassed. The overseas guys wait till they're in the toilets or somewhere out of sight before doing this.

The South African also enjoys making small talk with the petrol attendant, and will often ask him: 'Where did you learn to speak Afrikaans so well, hey, Baba?'

The waiter brings my Tafel, and then the guy next to me with the bush hat tries again to make conversation. 'Where are you headed?' he wants to know.

I end up telling him about oom Albertus, and that I like to wander through the Namib occasionally in search of myself.

He holds out a hand to me and introduces himself: Giep Oosthuizen. He's a borehole driller from Windhoek, but at the moment he's just wandering too, following the whirlwinds. He's just been through a rather messy divorce.

People sometimes say the most striking, truest things without being aware of it. After a while, after he's moved his bottle of Tafel in many more circles around his car keys, Giep says: 'Sometimes I wish I could find words for all the things I feel.'

This tends to happen when you wander through the desert: you experience everything around you very clearly, but the words to describe this keep slipping away, almost like a mirage in these vast open spaces.

I was five years old when I first arrived in the Namib. At the time, we lived in Grootfontein in the north of Namibia.

Namibia was then still South West and we stayed at the municipal resort at Swakop, my dad and my mom and I. I had a tiny fishing rod, a brown jersey, a multicoloured beach ball, and a yellow bucket and spade.

One afternoon my dad asked at a shop for a cardboard box for each of us, and we drove in the Valiant to the dunes. Then we clambered to the top of a dune, got into our cardboard boxes and slid all the way down to the bottom.

I still treasure a photo of my late mother sliding down the dune, smiling, her hair blowing in the wind.

Maybe one keeps returning to certain places in the hope, almost, of again meeting the person you used to be.

I'm now driving from Solitaire in the direction of Walvis Bay, sitting serenely behind the wheel of the Chico and mulling things over in my mind. How does Bruce Chatwin describe it, again? 'I was suspended in the beautiful solitude of the open road. There is a kind of introspection that only outdoor space generates, for inside and outside are more intertwined than the usual distinctions allow.'

On this side of Nauchas there is a turn-off to the left towards Gobabeb, Ururas and Rooibank, but I give it a miss. That road is too tough for a Chico. I take the C14 up to about 10 km before Walvis Bay, where another road turns off to Rooibank.

Here, between Walvis Bay and Rooibank, the earth is flat and white and filled with light. Can this stretch of nothing be called beautiful? Here the sun can burn you to a cinder by day and the same night you can be frozen to the marrow, because one thing is always true of the desert: everything happens on its terms.

Closer to Walvis Bay there is cellphone reception, because suddenly my phone rings in my trouser pocket. It's Johannes Bakkes, a writer and academic from Cape Town. 'Hello, pal,' he says. 'I've run away from home again. I'm at Maltahöhe. I'm going to the Namib.'

Bakkes, too, takes to wandering through the Namib whenever he starts feeling that he's no longer the calm and whole man he believes he ought to be.

How many such people haven't I encountered here in the Namib over the years? Johannes Bakkes and his brother Chrisjan, who's been living and wandering in Kaokoland north of here for donkey's years; Giep Oosthuizen, who I left a while ago at Solitaire, hunched over his Tafel lager; the late oom Pieter Pieterse, Laurie Raath from Uis and old Dries Boshoff with his clapped-out Land Rover, who sometimes searches for long periods for rare stones in the desert emptiness near the Brandberg.

You can easily spot them, these wanderers: many have long, wild beards and they're not inclined to talk much. You sometimes see them on their own in a bar in Henties Bay or Uis or Karibib or sitting at the tables in the Swakop bakery, or in an old bakkie or Land Rover parked somewhere out in the open. Often they just sit there and gaze into the distance as if the solution to all their problems lies somewhere on the horizon. Modern nomads, Bruce Chatwin calls them. People who keep wandering back on their own tracks.

It's now just past four in the afternoon; I'm about 35 km south of Walvis Bay, and ahead in the distance there is something shiny on the open veld. It's a corrugated iron shack. And then there's another one. And another.

Rooibank.

I paid my first visit to oom Albertus eight or nine years ago, after I'd read about him in Professor Hans du Plessis's book *Grensgeval*, which, among other things, deals with the different forms of Afrikaans.

Oom Albertus's father, Johannes, had arrived in Walvis Bay from the Cape early in the previous century. He fell in love with a local woman there, they married, and then trekked into the desert to settle here.

Only about a hundred people live here at Rooibank and they make a living mainly from narras, a pumpkin-like fruit that grows in the dry course of the Kuiseb. They are rugged desert people.

Hardly any tourists come here. Oom Albertus's hut stands apart on a slight incline next to the Kuiseb. I stop close by and get out of the car. A cool breeze wafts in from the direction of the sea. A dog is barking somewhere.

It feels as if this is exactly the place I should be now. I don't know why, but recently I've thought constantly about what oom Albertus once said: 'A person should totally be where he is,' he said

A person should totally be where he is.

The old man sometimes speaks in riddles like this, and if you question him too closely he's apt to say he wants to be alone, and then disappears among the reeds of the Kuiseb.

I walk towards the house. Outside, a crocheted patchwork quilt on the washing line stirs in the breeze. It sounds quiet inside. Here, in front of the door that cannot lock, oom Albertus and I have often sat drinking Kloof coffee and just being totally who we are.

The house has only two small rooms: a bedroom and a kitchen. I open the door and glance inside. No one. There's no kettle singing on the Dover as on some other occasions when I've visited Oom Albertus.

'Can I help you, Meneer?' a voice suddenly asks behind me.

I swing around. It's a man in an Edgars Club T-shirt.

'I'm looking for oom Albertus,' I say. 'Has the old man gone walk-about again?'

The man looks at me as if he feels sorry for me. 'Oom Albertus died two days ago, Meneer,' he replies. 'We're burying him on Saturday.'

The man introduces himself as Stephanus Bam, a nephew of oom Albertus. At this very moment they're digging the grave in the cemetery across the road. I accompany Stephanus to the site, but after a while I return to the house alone, as the spades scrape against the soil behind me.

I walk through oom Albertus's front door. Inside, it smells of a bit of everything: tobacco and coffee and soap and something that might be Jeyes Fluid.

Oom Albertus's bedroom, here where he died in his sleep two nights ago, is filled with the dignified poetry of poverty: a tin basin on the floor next to a pair of blue slippers, a jar of Vicks on a small table, a packet of Springbok tobacco, a bottle of pills from the clinic. And a suit hanging against the wall – a black suit on a wire hanger.

The desert gave and the desert took away.

I go outside again and sit down on one of the logs at the door. It's a brilliantly clear afternoon, and it's quiet, and all at once I am aware of everything around me: the red dunes in the distance, the anna-trees in the course of the Kuiseb, the five chickens and one Muscovy duck in the coop, the three-legged pot in which he sometimes cooked mealiepap. And suddenly everything is beautiful and peaceful and good.

But where will I go in future to be totally where I am?

Going back home in a Valiant

With the help of two petrol attendants at the BP garage in Oudtshoorn, I've been looking for the Valiant's petrol cap for the past five minutes – but we can't find it.

'Eish,' says the first one. 'Eisssh.'

'Maybe it's somewhere in the engine,' volunteers the other.

I pull the little lever under the steering wheel and open the bonnet. Nothing. We can't see an opening for the petrol tank anywhere.

Taking my cellphone from my pocket, I call Gerhard Stander, the bloke who'd sold me the Valiant. But his phone just rings.

'Hang on,' I say, 'just hang on.' I try to think. Way back then, when we had our Valiant, where did my dad put the petrol in?

That was a long time ago. Thirty-two years ago, to be precise. I was ten years old. In those days there were still Trek and Esso and Mobil garages, and petrol was 38c a litre. John Vorster was prime minister, Elvis was still officially alive, and the Valiant was one of the country's most popular cars.

We had an automatic 1973 Regal, identical to the one I've bought from Gerhard. My dad's was a bilious yellow colour; this one is a sort of Epol brown – the shade some people called 'shaki', a cross between shit and khaki.

Who doesn't have a Valiant somewhere in their past? Your dad had one, or your oupa, or perhaps that black sheep, perlemoen-poaching uncle from Gansbaai. Or your aunt, a wealthy widow from Newcastle who wore a fox-fur stole and smoked Rothmans through a long cigarette holder.

Sometimes the police, especially those in the detective branch, had an official Valiant, with a crackling two-way radio and a long, waving aerial attached to the back bumper.

Even some deputy government ministers had them. In 1972, Minister Louis le Grange, then deputy minister of justice, turned up at Daniëlskuil, the town of my youth, in a pitch-black Valiant VIP to give a speech at a Rapportryers' dinner.

I walk round to the back of the car, the attendants trailing be-hind me. Suddenly it hits me. The number plate . . . the number plate! The bloody petrol cap's behind the back number plate! How could I have forgotten?

I pull down the number plate, like a flap, and there it is.

'Eish,' says the attendant, and brings the fuel hose.

Suddenly I know: with this new, old car of mine I'm going to remember a lot of things I thought I'd forgotten.

Does the car you travelled in as a child influence the way you ex-perience the open road in later years? And if so, what effect did that yellow Valiant of my youth have on me?

With thoughts such as these in my head, I drive away from Oudtshoorn after filling up with 34,7 litres of petrol through the opening behind the number plate.

The N12 from Oudtshoorn to De Rust is level and free of potholes; ahead in the distance lies the Swartberg in its own shadow, and the Valiant's speedometer needle sways gently between 90–100 km/h. The gauges on these old cars tend to oscillate, as if they subtly want to draw your attention to the deteriorating shock absorbers.

Buying her was an impulsive decision. Three months earlier, when I was in Oudtshoorn for the arts festival, someone had told me that Gerhard was selling a Valiant that had belonged to his late father, Koos, a sometime stationmaster. I went to his house to have an idle look, just to see again the vehicle I'd more or less grown up in. There it stood, pregnant with memories.

Half an hour later, she was mine.

Oh, my Valiant wanted me, and now she had me.

I travelled down from Pretoria yesterday afternoon to collect her.

I'm still struggling a bit to find a comfortable driving position. Tackling the open road in an unfamiliar car is a bit like getting to know a new lover. You first have to get used to the contours of each others' bodies. It feels as though I'm sitting too deep down in the seat – I can hardly see the little round badge at the far end of the bonnet that looks like the peep sight on a Lee-Enfield .303. And when I rest my elbow on the door, with the window open, I can't quite reach the roof outside to drum on it with my fingers.

I lean forward and turn on the radio, but it doesn't work. Perhaps, though, silence is the right accompaniment for an introspective pilgrimage; a journey into yourself.

The family's yellow Valiant also had a radio – a Supersonic. Or was it a Blaupunkt? I remember that often, between towns, the radio would produce nothing more than a stubborn hiss. In those days, you still depended on the occasional FM-masts for radio reception. At Mobil garages you could even get free maps of South Africa indicating the places that had FM-masts by means of a large red dot.

Later, my dad installed a Hitachi cassette player under the dashboard, in a sort of wooden box that oom Gielie Swiegers had made for him. He also covered the front seats with sheepskin seat covers. Why is it that nobody has sheepskin seat covers in their cars any more?

Luckily, De Rust is still 10 km away, because I'm wandering through the labyrinth of my memories, passing one ostrich farm after another.

I run my eyes over the gauges and lights in front of me on the dashboard: the petrol tank is full, the odometer tells me my chariot has travelled 112 699 miles, the clock stopped at eleven minutes to three on some or other day, and the temperature gauge's red needle hovers a whisker above normal.

What was it my dad said when the needle sat in that spot? 'She's running a little hot.'

We travelled this same road in our yellow Valiant years ago, but in the opposite direction. To Hartenbos.

People with Valiant Regals liked to holiday at Hartenbos. Or on the Natal South Coast, or any place that had hot springs: Aliwal North, Badplaas, Goudini or Warmbaths, where many of the men would arrive at the pool on the first day of their holiday with red sunburn all the way up the right arm, because that arm had rested on the Valiant's rolled-down window frame the entire journey.

But there were Valiants to suit other tastes and pockets, too. There was also the Rebel, the VIP and the Charger.

The VIP was for those who wanted comfort and style – and could afford it. In 1973 it would set you back about R5 000. It had power steering and chrome hubcaps and, most important, a vinyl top. In fact, all this meant was that the roof was covered with a sort of stick-on imitation leather, but it gave the car the same cachet that a cabriolet enjoys today.

The Valiant Charger was a flatter, wider, sportier-looking model, fitted with a rev counter, not something commonly seen in cars of the time. Serious petrolheads would sometimes buy a rev counter and fit it at home, usually on top of the dashboard, at an angle next to the steering wheel.

The Regal didn't really have much in the way of luxuries, except that it was fitted with an item that was considered a revolutionary piece of technology in those days – an automatic choke.

This meant that, on cold mornings, you no longer had to hook two fingers behind an old-fashioned choke knob, pull it, and manipulate the thing with painstaking care so as not to flood the engine. In the Valiant, incredibly, it was all done for you.

Even so, not everyone greeted the automatic choke with equal enthusiasm.

'Nah, it's a piece of rubbish,' they'd say. 'It just gets stuck and pushes up your fuel consumption.' Some ooms would even remove their Valiant's automatic choke and fit a standard, manual one in its place.

I've just pulled up at the only garage in De Rust and asked the attendant to check the water level. A man crosses the road and introduces himself: Dougie van Wyngaardt.

'Hello, Boet,' he says, caressing the old car with his eyes. 'Where did you get this one? She's still spotless.'

'I bought her in Oudtshoorn, Oom,' I reply.

Suddenly I realise I'm starting to sound like my dad and all the other ooms who owned Valiants. They invariably referred to them in the feminine, as 'her' or 'she'. 'She's running a bit hot,' they would say, or 'She needs a wash.' Sometimes one would come up to our car at a filling station and say, 'Excuse me, sir – if you don't mind my asking – how much does she give you?'

During the exchange my mother would sit coolly next to my father, engrossed in a Mills and Boon novel – she knew that the stranger was referring to the Valiant, wanting to establish its petrol consumption.

Oom Dougie and I watch from a safe distance as the petrol attendant opens the bonnet to inspect the radiator. The Valiant's radiator cap isn't just a little plastic thing set safely on one side, as in today's cars. It's a no-nonsense steel cap, set squarely in the middle of the radiator top. If you unscrew it too quickly, you're likely to be scalded by a jet of boiling water.

Cloth in hand, the attendant loosens the cap carefully, almost as if he's defusing a bomb.

'Careful, now . . . slowly,' warns oom Dougie. 'Slo-o-owly!'

213

A jet of steam shoots from the opening. The attendant keeps his hand on the radiator, but plants his feet as far back from the Valiant as possible. Then he gives the cap one final, fearless turn. It comes off, but no water sprays out because there wasn't enough left in the radiator.

The attendant fetches a watering can while oom Dougie stares at the engine as if it's a long-lost friend.

'Straight six,' he says, with something like nostalgia in his voice. 'Straight six.'

Indeed, this is a six-cylinder engine, 3,8 litres. With electronic ignition. (Or so it says on the sticker on the back window.)

'In my day I had a Barracuda,' oom Dougie says, shaking his head and letting out a long whistle. 'I'm telling you, that car could move, ou broer!'

The first Valiants appeared on South African roads in the early 1960s. They were made by the American manufacturer Chrysler at a plant in Elsies River in Cape Town, and the Barracuda was one of the first models. It had an enormous, sharply angled rear window, and in some models the spare wheel was fitted on the outside, on top of the boot.

'Not your kid brother's car', was the Barracuda's marketing slogan.

Somebody once said that going round a sharp corner in a Valiant was like sitting on the back of an elephant trying to balance on golf balls.

I'm still on the N12, about 10 km other side of De Rust, driving through the crags of Meiringspoort in the direction of Beaufort West. And let's be honest here: she's perhaps not quite a wobbly elephant, but she doesn't exactly stick to the road through these curves like Jody Scheckter's Tyrrell Ford with its six wheels.

My imagination takes me back to one of those trips to Hartenbos in the old yellow Valiant. I remember feeling sick in the car somewhere around here.

Do people still get carsick, I wonder, especially on winding roads with bends like these in Meiringspoort? Or did people only get carsick in big, rocking cars like Valiants?

It's something you used to see often: someone next to a parked car at the side of the road, bending over, sick as a dog.

People would try all sorts of things to avoid getting carsick. They took pills and also made sure they had 'something in their stomach' before going on a journey.

At one stage my father tried another cure for the carsickness that plagued my mother and me. To the underside of the car he attached a short length of chain, which dragged on the road. In those days thousands of cars were similarly equipped. The chain was supposed to reduce static electricity, which in turn had an effect on the carbon levels in your bloodstream. Or something like that.

We also never took to the open road without a water bag. Dad bolted a little iron bar to the bumper – next to the AA badge – to hang the water bag on. (My dad was an AA man, not a Rondalia man.)

The bag in question was made of heavy canvas, and it had a spout with a cork in it. My dad would stop at a cement picnic table in the shade of an old pepper tree somewhere along the road and we'd drink the cool water straight from the bag as the telephone wires sang and all around the world quivered in the haze.

The Valiant sways through Meiringspoort, past Spookdrif, Herriese-klip, Ontploffingsdrif and Pereboomdrif.

Klaarstroom. Still about 100 km to Beaufort West, and in the rear-view mirror the Swartberg range grows smaller as the Great Karoo unfolds before me.

Now my Valiant is a ship on a calm sea on a clear morning. Or that's what I sometimes imagined in days gone by when we set out in the yellow Valiant from Daniëlskuil – that I was sailing on the open sea.

You're sitting there on the back seat, your dad whistling a tune behind the steering wheel, your mother immersed in a Mills and Boon or a Catherine Cookson novel and laughing now and then, as the family voyage slowly into the open seas of the Northern Cape on the way to Hartenbos, the Natal South Coast, the Holiday-on-Ice show in Kimberley, or wherever.

You hear the drone of the engine and the song of the tyres on the tar. A Heino cassette plays in the Hitachi, and the wind whistles through the small window on your mother's side – the one that doesn't close properly. Outside, the khaki-coloured bushes and aloes and windmills slide past you and the world seems huge all around you.

Then you get sleepy and stretch out on the seat. For a while you look up at the telephone lines dipping and rising outside the window between the poles, up and down, up and down, before you fall asleep.

While I'm thinking about all these things, I suddenly notice something in my rear-view mirror. It's a car – a Cortina? Uh-huh, looks like an XR6, a 'fat six'.

Almost instinctively, I hit the accelerator. The Trimatic gearbox automatically kicks down to second, and the speedometer needle starts creeping towards 120 km/h. Then there's a slight jolt as she changes back into third.

'Did you feel her kicking down?' my dad sometimes asked when he floored our Valiant like that. 'Did you feel that?'

Okay, okay, the Cortina won. It overtook me. But I did keep up with it for, well, about five hundred metres before it roared off and disappeared into the mirage on the horizon.

A Valiant isn't built for speed, you see.

A Valiant is a dream, a time machine, a way of reminding yourself who you once were. Or that's how it feels to me at the moment, anyway.

I've just driven into Beaufort West, and stopped at a red traffic light. On the pavement stands a man wearing a Powerhouse Blue

Bulls T-shirt. He looks at my Valiant with a huge grin, and when the light turns green, he shouts loudly: *'Steek hom, pappa! Steek hom!'* (Which I take to mean: Go for it, mate!)

Many people react like this when they see a Valiant: they smile.

Do they smile for the same reason you smile when you see those black-and-white pictures of Springbok rugby players from decades ago? Does a Valiant with its cumbersome bodywork look just as odd and out of place today as those rugby players in their heavy boots and long, wide shorts?

Or do they smile because they recognise something of themselves in the car?

We all have our own Valiant memories: long drives to seaside holidays, nights at the drive-in, four people on the back seat . . .

As an only child, I had the whole back seat of the yellow Valiant to myself. But people who come from large families will tell you all sorts of stories about the politics on a Valiant's back seat: the arguments about who sits at the door, who sits in the middle, who sits in front between Ma and Pa. While Pa threatens: 'If you lot don't shut up now, I'll drop you all off right here!'

I pull up outside the Squires Loft in Donkin Street, Beaufort's main road. My friend Gert, who lives in the town, is waiting for me there. He comes up to the car together with another local resident, Frik Botha, a former heavyweight boxer.

They walk around the Valiant, and stop at the boot. 'Look how white she still burns,' remarks Gert, pointing to the exhaust pipe.

He's right. The inside of the exhaust is a light grey colour.

I've never been entirely sure why this was the case, but apparently your engine was healthy if your exhaust 'burns white'.

My dad and various other Valiant owners were constantly peering at one another's exhausts and having conversations like this:

'She's burning a bit black, isn't she?'

'Looks like it, yes.'

'What do you think it is? Rings?'

'No, no – I think it's just her timing that's probably out.'

With the arrival of unleaded petrol, everything changed. All cars using it now 'burn black'. But the LRP (lead replacement petrol) I use still gives the exhaust pipe a hint of a healthy, light grey hue.

As we sit at a sunlit table in front of the Squires Loft, it's as if the Valiant has dislodged the disputes of times gone by. Soon we have a heated debate about a very old bone of contention: who was the better boxer, Gerrie Coetzee or Kallie Knoetze? In the 1970s, you were either a Kallie man or a Gerrie man, in the same way as you shouted for either the Blue Bulls or Western Province, or believed Abba's Anni-Frid was sexier by far than Agnetha.

But Frik has the last word. As an amateur, he fought against both Gerrie and Kallie, and both of them had beaten him. He stares at us from beneath heavy eyebrows. 'Gerrie,' he says. 'Gerrie donnered me harder.' He points to our glasses. 'Come on, drink up. I feel like a Sunday afternoon drive.'

In Daniëlskuil we always used to go for a Sunday afternoon drive in the Valiant, though the town was really too small for a proper drive. My dad would buy us each a Zoom ice-cream at oom Mike's café, and we'd park at the side of the Kimberley road, eat the ice-creams, and watch the cars that passed by. A few Chev 4.1s, a Toyopet Stout bakkie or two, and perhaps even a Citroën Pallas, a rare sight in those days.

Now Gert, Frik and I are in the Valiant, heading towards the hill that rises on the eastern side of the town. 'Go that way,' says Gert, pointing to a road next to the Apostolic Faith Mission.

A rough track straggles up the side of the hill, but the Valiant manages it easily. We stop at the top, next to a white trig beacon. You don't get beacons like that any more. When they fall down, they don't rebuild them. The advent of GPS has made them redundant.

We get out of the car. Below us, to the right, lies the town dam, and behind us the Valiant's engine tick-ticks as it cools down. Whenever I hear that sound, I think of Oupa. He and Ouma sometimes joined us when we went on holiday in the bilious yellow Valiant.

It was usually still dark when we left the house early in the morning; by ten o'clock we were well on our way. That was when the morning service was broadcast on Radio South Africa, and no matter where we were at the time, my dad always pulled over and stopped. Oupa would take off his hat with its leopard-skin band, and the Valiant would tick and creak irreverently while the minister prayed.

Gert, Frik and I stare in silence at a passing jet's contrail curving across the blue vault of the sky. Then Frik gets back into the Valiant, lights a cigarette and sprawls there as if he's relaxing on a Gomma Gomma sofa. Somewhere a church bell rings. To the south, in the direction of the township, a blanket of smog hangs low over the dusty earth.

'Do you know that poem by NP van Wyk Louw where he writes about wanting to stand once again at the town dam at twilight?' Gert asks after a while. 'They say this dam was supposed to have inspired it.'

How do you do this again? Do you divide the number of litres of petrol you've put in the car by the number of kilometres you've driven? Or is it the other way round?

It's the next morning. I spent the night at Gert's, and having filled the tank again, I'm trying to calculate the Valiant's fuel consumption.

In the old days, practically everyone had one of those little logbooks in the cubbyhole where they did their calculations. My dad sometimes also did them in the small brown leatherette Volkskas diary he kept in his top pocket along with his Parker pen.

I divide the litres into the kilos and get the answer: 8,7 km per litre.

That's not too bad. Especially considering that we had a head wind. And it's quite a big car. And she needs a service. And the front tyres are a bit smooth. And also, she's got that automatic choke ...

As I get back in and settle behind the wheel, I hear a voice out-side: 'I hope you've got a spare fan belt with you.'

It's Thys, a lorry driver, who has wandered up to have a closer look at the Valiant. He's only joking about the fan belt but, even so, my dad and the other Valiant ooms would never have gone on a long trip without one.

My dad did make that mistake once, and the Valiant's fan belt broke somewhere in the wide open spaces outside Kimberley. He had to ask Ouma, the only one in the car wearing stockings: 'Mammie, would you mind taking off your stockings?'

Back then, stockings were a good temporary replacement for a fan belt.

Most Valiant owners would never have left home without a container of water and a complete tool kit – especially not for this stretch of road from Beaufort West to Colesberg. In their minds, this desolate piece of the world would swallow you up if you weren't properly prepared.

Valiant drivers would never go anywhere, either, without an empty container (for petrol) and a piece of garden hose (to siphon petrol out of another vehicle). It's rather strange, if you think about it. Why didn't they just fill the container with petrol and take it along like that?

I say goodbye to Thys and head north on the N1, in the direction of Three Sisters. Already I feel more comfortable in my low posi-tion behind the wheel. There's just one thing I still find hard to get used to: a Valiant doesn't allow you to forget about the world around you. You always hear the road under you, and air always comes in from somewhere.

This is no longer the case in today's cars, with their soundproof interiors.

Also, instead of having those small triangular front windows that opened separately, everything's just one big window now. I don't think I've ever been in a Valiant where the side windows didn't start whistling disconsolately at anything above 80 km/h.

My dad always put ice-cream sticks between the latch and the frame to try and silence it, but it never worked for long.

With the side window whistling away, I drift slowly past Nelspoort and Three Sisters, to www.richmond.co.za. Well, that's the name spelt out these days in whitewashed stones on the koppie outside the town.

Has Richmond's name also changed, I wonder, and stop at the Caltex garage near the road. 'No, Meneer,' one of the petrol attendants reassures me. 'See, Meneer, we're also on the Internet now.'

I buy some springbok biltong at the local butchery, and head for Colesberg. The N1 isn't what you might call a Valiant-friendly road. There are far too many trucks and speeding officials in government cars on their way to emergency meetings or municipal imbizos in places like Trompsburg and De Aar.

So I turn off the N1 at Colesberg, onto the R58, which passes the Gariep Dam on the way to Bethulie. All of a sudden, about 3 km from Bethulie, I hear a loud scraping noise coming from somewhere towards the back of the car. Still, I press on into the town, past a sign that proclaims: *We love our children*.

Near what was once Bethulie's Royal Hotel is a workshop – General Repair Services – where guys in blue overalls bustle about busily. I pull up outside, get out of the car without bothering to close the door again, and walk round to the boot. Bending down, I see what is causing the scraping noise. The exhaust pipe has come loose, and is dragging on the ground.

Two men walk up to me, Oelof Cahldo and Trevor Carter, with Brutus the dachshund a few steps behind them. All three start inspecting the Valiant.

Trevor pulls the Valiant up onto the hoist, lifts it up and stands under her. Then he gives two low whistles. Is there anyone who can whistle more ominously than a mechanic?

What now? you immediately think when you hear it. How bad is it? What will it cost?

'Don't worry,' says Trevor. 'It's just the rubbers that are finished.'

Workshops like Oelof and Trevor's are also becoming scarcer these days. Many mechanics (or what do they call themselves nowadays? Vehicle technicians?) don't even work in overalls any more. Spanners hang in orderly rows on General Repair Services' wall, each with its position and outline precisely marked in a felt-tipped pen. To the right of them is a dusty calendar with a photo of Table Mountain. And there are also Wynne's and STP stickers, and the business card of a radiator specialist named Nicky McMinnie.

Behind a glass partition on Oelof's desk stands a Goodyear ashtray – one of those old ones you used to get with a small rubber tyre around it.

How long will you still see decor like this?

'No, no, it's not necessary,' says Oelof once they've finished with the car and I try to pay. 'It was only two little rubber bands.'

Two little rubber bands and new memories.

Trevor laughs. 'There's just one thing I want to tell you,' he says. 'Sorry, Brutus stole your biltong from the car and ate it.'

Perhaps this is some strange kind of revenge, I think, because in 1974 my dad in his Valiant accidentally ran over tant Sannie Grové's dachshund, Snippie, and killed it.

At first I'd planned to travel from Bethulie to Pretoria through the eastern Free State, past Smithfield, Dewetsdorp and Winburg. But I've changed my mind, and am now aiming that little round badge on the Valiant's nose towards the north-west.

I'm driving past Trompsburg, Jagersfontein and Kimberley towards Ventersdorp – the town in the old Western Transvaal where my retired father has been living for the last couple of years.

I've decided that my dad should have a chance to see the world again through the windows of a Valiant.

In my trouser pocket, I keep a little notebook where I jot down all sorts of things: random observations, the names of people and places, things that I hear or read about and want to remember. In the front of the book is a quote from the American travel writer

Barry Lopez. 'The best of us find a measure of wisdom, enlighten-
ment and self-fulfillment through constant travel,' Lopez writes.
'The worst of us are fleeing from ourselves, and most of us strike
a wavering course somewhere in between.'

In the past few days I've looked at it several times, because the
Valiant has made me aware of things that I haven't always seen
too clearly before. You see archaic motor car workshops, and kudu
horns displayed against the walls of front stoeps, and in front of
some houses you see walls with ox-wagon patterns etched into
the cement, you see miniature windmills and plaster gnomes and
golf ball postboxes in gardens. You also see deserted grounds where
the Day of the Vow used to be celebrated, and cement strips in
town squares where oxen and men in velskoene had walked during
the symbolic 1938 ox-wagon trek.

In Warrenton you discover that there are others in this country
with Valiant memories of their own – people who inhabit a world
you know very little about. I've just stopped at the BP garage in
the town, and Shorty Dibetso is telling me how he used to travel
from here to visit his brother in Johannesburg – in a Valiant.

'All our taxis used to be Valiants,' recalls Shorty. 'They loaded
those cars. They really loaded them full, Makosi.'

Shorty himself lived in Johannesburg for a while, and he remembers that there were Valiant taxis there too.

For people like Shorty, a Valiant wasn't just a comfortable car
that was a pleasure to own and drive, as it was for me. Instead, it
was more like a lifeboat. He looks at me, and then asks the inevi-
table question. 'You're not selling this one, are you, Makosi?"

I shake my head. 'Sorry, brother, it's not for sale.' And then I
remember something. Each time before we left on holiday in the
yellow Valiant, heading for the coast, our gardener, Simon, would
hand over an empty oil can with the request that we fill it with sea
water and bring it back for him. 'It's good for the stomach,' he
would say.

Once, though, we forgot, and on the way home, passing through

223

Barkly West, we guiltily remembered. We filled the can with ordinary tap water, and added two packets of Cerebos table salt.

When did my dad sell our Valiant? Was it in '80? Or in '82, as more and more petrol attendants began asking him if he didn't want to sell the car?

There was a time when such approaches by petrol attendants were a bit of an embarrassment, a strong indication that it was time to trade the car in for something more modern.

But I suppose my dad sold it in the end for the same reason everyone else did – because newer and better models with improved fuel consumption and all kinds of other refinements had appeared on the market. The last Valiants were manufactured in 1980. After that, Chrysler officially ceased its operations in South Africa.

It's now about half past three in the afternoon and I'm close to Ventersdorp.

'The Prodigal Son,' I say to myself, 'has come home. In a Valiant.'

I pull up on the pavement outside the house, and hoot. The dogs come barking to the gate and my father appears on the stoep, rather bent in his grey Grasshoppers, leaning on his kierie. The old legs are a bit shaky these days. He is, after all, seventy-five years old.

I stand next to the Valiant, throw my arms wide, and say, 'What do think of her, Pa?'

He shuffles impatiently across the lawn. 'My boy, my boy, my boy,' he says, and caresses the Valiant's bonnet with a trembling hand. For some reason he doesn't open the door, but looks in through the back window with his hand shading his eyes, like a small boy looking in a shop window.

'Get in, Pa, go on.'

'My boy, my boy, my boy.'

Once again I get in behind the wheel. My dad puts his kierie in the car, bends forward with difficulty, then half tumbles onto the seat, with his Grasshoppers in the air.

I start the engine – chi-chi-chi – and off we go.

'My boy, my boy, my boy – she goes beautifully.'

We just drive. In my imagination, there's a wicker basket at my father's feet, with two Thermos flasks of coffee and a Tupperware lunch box in case we get hungry. Inside the lunch box there are sausages, meatballs, a few hard-boiled eggs, tomato sandwiches. And a jammerlappie, too, since I don't want any grease stains on my Valiant.

We drive down the main street of Ventersdorp, past the Standard Bank and the dry-cleaners, where two Pakistanis now run a shop where you can get anything from an umbrella to a pair of genuine imitation Nike trainers.

We drive past the chemist and Jannie's barbershop, with its notice on the door: *We sharpen scissors*. These days there's a satellite dish on the roof of the Madeira café, and they're even planning a golf estate for the town.

We drive out of the town, Pa and I, past my late mother's grave in the cemetery and the deserted railway station and the grain silos. I look in the rear-view mirror and imagine that oom Koos Stander, the stationmaster who bought the old car 'out of the box' in 1973, is sitting on the back seat – he and Oupa with his leopard-skin hat, and my aunt from Newcastle who smoked Rothmans in a cigarette holder. Oh, and for good measure, Snippie, tant Sannie's departed dachshund, too.

We don't talk much, Pa and me. We just drive, out into the green, open spaces, listening to the engine and feeling every little bump and hump in the road under us, sitting peacefully like the lion and the lamb, comfortably cushioned in the old Valiant's front seat.

This landscape is written in a sort of Braille, which a Valiant can easily read.

I am an African

Without the hills and the valleys, the mountains and the marshes, the rivers and the deserts, the trees and the flowers of this continent, I am not I.

This is where I shiver with cold, and where the sun beats down on me. This is where I cling to a lamp post when the south-easter blows in Cape Town, where I am drenched in the rain, and cover the mirror in my bedroom with a blanket when there's thunder – just as my late grandmother did, and my great-grandmother, and all the generations before them.

This is where I am happy and where I am furious, where I laugh and I am sad, where I believe, I pray, I hope, I fear, I doubt, I curse, I despair.

Sometimes I try to forget events that took place here in the past – events that, if you remember them, serve as a warning against losing your humanity.

Bloukrans, Bethulie, Bulhoek, Boipatong.

Abraham Esau, Jopie Fourie, Bessie Head, Lucky Dube, and oom Sarel Breedt who was murdered on his farm Honingskrans in the Roossenekal district the other day. This is where I try to love and try to forgive.

Documents in the Cape archives show that my ancestors came from Europe, but their cathedrals, palaces and villas became forts, gabled houses and hartbeeshuisies on this soil. And the blood of Malay slaves and Khoi women who harvested buchu in the veld near Garies flows in my veins too, and, like them, I believe in the spirits of the ancestors: Shaka, Oom Lokomotief, De la Rey and De Wet, Nat Nakasa, and my oupa Danie, with his cackling little laugh.

I don't want to live in Australia, Canada or Britain, even though you don't have to lock your doors there at night, even though you can still have a South African church, a South African newspaper, South African chutney, a South African dentist and a South African gynaecologist in those parts.

All that I am and know is entwined with this glorious, merciless corner of the world where I was born in sin, screaming, at two-thirty one morning.

This is where I see TV images of dead dogs, dead cattle with severed hamstrings, dead children with dead smiles, dead policemen, dead mothers, and fathers lying dead on pavements after bank robberies.

But this is also where I see dreams and business plans come to life, where I see signs of grace, and dads and moms smiling proudly for cameras in Spur restaurants after graduation ceremonies. Tabloid newspapers don't report on faith, people don't phone Niekie van den Berg's radio talk show *Sê wie?* and wax lyrical about hope, and *Carte Blanche* has never done an exposé on love.

Those who look with compassionate eyes shall be granted grace.

I am related to a leopard and a mamba and all the donkeys in the Colesberg district. I am buchu, saltbush and tambotie, puddingstone and tiger's eye and tanzanite. I am the Limpopo and the Zambezi, the Congo and the Lualaba and the Nile, because I have crossed a Rubicon in my heart.

I am an African.

Glossary

7de Laan	Popular Afrikaans TV soap opera
Afrikaanse Christelike Vrouevereniging (ACVV)	Afrikaans Christian women's organisation, known for it's charitable work
Bakens	Beacons, landmarks
Baster	Literally 'bastard', derogatory term for a person of mixed race. However, used without any negative connotation by certain groups in Namibia and South Africa as part of their name as a people or a community (e.g. Bosluis Basters)
Bedonnerd	Moody, cantankerous
Blommetjie	Little flower, often used as an endearment
Bodorp	The upper part of a town; used figuratively to denote the wealthier part of a town (in contrast to the poorer 'onder dorp')
Boerebarok	Pretentious architectural styles favoured by Afrikaans-speaking people with more money than taste (literally 'boer baroque')
Boet	Form of address used by older men towards younger men (*see* Broer)
Bokkoms	Salted and dried mullet; fish biltong
Bokwa	Buck wagon (humorous)
Bossie	Small indigenous bushes
Bosveldbul	Bushveld bull; figuratively, a tough guy from the Bushveld
boytjies	Variant form of 'boys'; used when addressing a group of boys/men
Bggroer	*See* Broer
Broer	Form of address equivalent to brother, mate, old chap, man. Other forms are 'ou broer' (with 'ou' meaning old) or 'bggroer', spelt thus to indicate the pronunciation when the speaker talks with a burr

Diener	Old-fashioned regional word for policeman
Donnered	Past tense of 'donner', i.e. to beat up, wallop or thrash someone
Duusman	White man (obsolete)
Dwaal	To roam or wander
Frikkadelle	Meatballs (diminutive: frikkadelletjies)
Halley-sê-kom-eet	Literally 'Halley says come and eat', a play on 'Halley se komeet' (Halley's Comet)
Hardegat	Stubborn
Hartbeeshuisies	Wattle and daub huts
Hartseer	Heartsore, sad
Herberg	Inn
Jammerlappie	Finger cloth
Jannie-verjaar-koeldrank	Literally 'Jannie's birthday cool drink' – a cool drink typically served at a children's birthday party
Jol	To party or have fun; to play (e.g. jol rugby)
Jong	Coloured male servant (obsolete and derogatory)
Jou kant	Your side (e.g. your side of the story or the argument)
Kambro	Edible plant found in the arid Karoo and the Hantam
Karretjie	Donkey cart
Kiekie	Snapshot, photograph
Kloof	Ravine, gorge
Koekoes	Mad
Kontrepsie	Contraption, device
Laaitie	Young boy
Lanie	White man, boss, member of a wealthy class
Lekker	Nice, pleasant, enjoyable
Mampoer	Home-made peach brandy
Manne	Men

Meisie	Young girl
Meneer	Sir
Moerse	Very big
Mos	As you know
Noot vir noot	Popular TV musical quiz show with a studio audience
Ogies	An instruction to people to close their eyes before grace is said at a meal. (literally 'little eyes', as the instruction is mostly directed at children)
Onderdorp	The lower, poorer part of town *see* Bodorp
Ool	Shortened form of 'oolfant' (olifant), regional word for elephant
Oolfant	Elephant *see* Ool
Oom	Literally 'uncle', but also used to address men older than oneself in South African country towns and rural areas; 'an oom' (diminutive: 'oompie') sometimes denotes 'a man'
Oom Lokomotief	Alias of Daniel Francois du Toit (1846-1923), pioneer Afrikaans journalist and campaigner for the development of Afrikaans as a written language. For fourteen years he was editor of *Die Afrikaanse Patriot* (which first appeared in 1876).
Ou beesblaas	Literally 'old cow's bladder'; sometimes used as a term of endearment
Ou broer	Literally 'old brother' *see* Broer
Ou maat	Literally 'old friend'; mate, old chap.
Ou swaer	Literally 'old brother-in-law'; used as a form of address among males who are not related (similar to old chap, old pal, etc.)
Ouma	Grandmother
Ounooi	Missus, (old) mistress (obsolete)
Oupa	Grandfather
Patatboer	Sweet-potato farmer
Perlemoen	Abalone

Platteland	The country districts of South Africa; rural as opposed to urban areas
Poort	Literally a gate, entrance or gateway; as a geographical feature, the word refers to a pass
Rapportryers	Afrikaans cultural organisation
Seun	Boy, son, lad
Siejy!	Go/get away! (Said to a dog)
Sinkietjie	Small piece of corrugated iron
Skuinskoeke	Literally 'skew cakes', a type of pastry cake
Slapgat	A person who is lazy; a slacker or a quitter
Sommer	Just, merely, for no particular reason
Spiekeries	Smart, snazzy; hunky-dory
Syntoe	That way, there (regional form of 'soontoe', i.e. 'that way or there')
Tannie	Aunt or auntie (used interchangeably with 'tant' or 'tante' as a form of address in country areas; tannie or tante can also denote woman)
Tant/Tante	Aunt *see* Tannie
Tier	Tiger, though often used in Afrikaans to refer to a leopard
Velskoene	Shoes made of rawhide
Vetkoek	A deep-fried bread ball that can be eaten in a variety of ways (e.g. with a savoury meat filling, or buttered, with jam or honey)
Vlei	Marshy area
Vrouediens	A women's organisation (literally 'women's service')
Wys jou muis	Encouragement to a stripper to reveal all (vulgar)
Zol	Hand-rolled cigarette

ABOUT THE AUTHOR

DANA SNYMAN was born in Stellenbosch, the son of a church minister who frequently uprooted his family to follow a calling to yet another remote little town.

Many moves later, Dana matriculated in Nylstroom (now Modimolle) and after a brief and unsuccessful stint at university, worked variously as a security guard, switchboard operator and bookshop clerk.

He stumbled into journalism by fortunate coincidence, initially as crime reporter for *Beeld*, and later at *Huisgenoot* where he covered everything from bomb explosions to the world *kettie*-shooting championships. In 2004, he became travel writer at *Weg* magazine.

Dana writes columns, plays and scripts and supports WP. His previous books, *Uit die binneland*, *Anderkant die scrap* and *Waar die leeus Afrikaans verstaan*, a *Weg* anthology to which he contributed, are top-sellers. *On the Back Roads* is his first book to be published in English.

When he is not on the road, Dana lives in Cape Town.